The
Entrepreneur's
Book of Checklists

FUEL^{RCA}

PEARSON
Prentice Hall
BUSINESS

Books that make you better

Books that make you better. That make you *be* better, *do* better, *feel* better. Whether you want to upgrade your personal skills or change your job, whether you want to improve your managerial style, become a more powerful communicator, or be stimulated and inspired as you work.

Prentice Hall Business is leading the field with a new breed of skills, careers and development books. Books that are a cut above the mainstream – in topic, content and delivery – with an edge and verve that will make you better, with less effort.

Books that are as sharp and smart as you are.

Prentice Hall Business.
We work harder – so you don't have to.

For more details on products, and to contact us, visit
www.pearsoned.co.uk

The Entrepreneur's Book of Checklists

1000 tips to help you start and grow your business

2nd Edition

Robert Ashton

PEARSON
Prentice Hall
BUSINESS

London • New York • Toronto • Sydney • Tokyo • Singapore
Hong Kong • Cape Town • Madrid • Paris • Amsterdam • Munich • Milan

PEARSON EDUCATION LIMITED

Edinburgh Gate
Harlow CM20 2JE
Tel: +44 (0)1279 623623
Fax: +44 (0)1279 431059
Website: www.pearsoned.co.uk

First published 2004
Second edition published in Great Britain 2007

© Pearson Education Limited 2004, 2007

The right of Robert Ashton to be identified as Author
of this Work has been asserted by him in accordance
with the Copyright, Designs and Patents Act 1988.

ISBN 978-0-273-71290-9

British Library Cataloguing in Publication Data
A CIP catalogue record for this book can be obtained from the British Library.

10 9 8 7 6 5 4 3 2 1
11 10 09 08 07

Cartoon illustrations by Andrzej Krauze
Typeset in 11pt/13¼pt Berkley by 3

Printed and bound in Great Britain by Ashford Colour Press Ltd., Gosport

The Publisher's policy is to use paper manufactured from sustainable forests.

This book is dedicated to my wife Belinda, my son Tom and my daughter Ruth. Entrepreneurship is exciting, stimulating and rewarding, but almost impossible without the support of a loving family. However hard you work at starting and growing your enterprise, always make time for your family.

Contents

Introduction

This book provides practical tips and advice for anybody who wants to start or grow a business. First published in 2004, thousands of enterprising people have already found it a valuable, easy to read guide. However, since 2004 the business world has changed. We are doing more business online, social enterprise is becoming increasingly important and we are even more acutely environmentally aware.

In this second edition you will find a greater emphasis on the role of the internet, case studies from the social, as well as the 'for profit', sector and some useful document templates that you can adapt and use. Here are ten good reasons for reading further.

1. **Ideas** – sometimes the desire to start or grow a business is there but the killer idea is not. This book shows you how to generate and test your business ideas.

2. **Wealth** – your own business may sound appealing but should you give up the security of employment? Read how to make the decision: full-time, part-time or not at all!

3. **Goals** – what do you really want from your business? See how setting lifestyle goals will help you focus your business vision.

4. **Capital** – finding the money is never simple, but this book lists places to look that you've probably never thought of. The bank is not your only option!

5. **More customers** – if your business is not growing, it's probably shrinking! Find out how to manage the flow of new business and keep control of your sales and your profits.

6. **Visibility** – the easier your product or service is to find, the more frequently people will contact you. Discover how marketing needn't cost much money at all.

7. **Time** – you're running so fast you can't stop. Learn how to manage your time and how to recruit people to help you and to manage them effectively.

8. **Payment** – do people keep you waiting? Cash flow is the lifeblood of any growing business. This book gives you new ways to make sure you always get paid.

9. **Internet** – a website alone will not deliver the business you are seeking. Find out how to use the internet wisely and successfully.

10. **Exit** – at some point you'll want to cash in and sell up. This book tells you how.

This book is a practical guide to the many challenges you may face when you plan, start, grow and sell your business. Each checklist gives you ten key points to consider or tips to try. Some will seem obvious and others obscure. All, however, can help you succeed.

This book is written for busy people who want a shortcut to inspiration and ideas. It is perfect for you if you:

- want to start your own business;
- have a small business and want it to grow;
- are studying business and want a practical book that says how it's done;
- manage a charity or social enterprise and want to become more sustainable;
- advise small business owners and want a handy, no nonsense guide;
- teach people about enterprise in all its forms;
- find business books hard to read – this book is very accessible and easy to read;
- live with someone growing a business who needs help;
- sell to small businesses and want to understand what's important to them;
- are smart enough to buy books that deliver value for money straight away!

There are many case studies throughout the book. All are based on real people, although some have asked for their names to be changed.

Why you should also seek business advice

national federation of
enterprise agencies

It should come as no surprise to discover that people who receive help and advice as they establish and grow their business are more successful than those who don't. Studies by Barclays show that small business start-ups are 20% more likely to succeed if they seek help from an Enterprise Agency. Reading books like this one can also improve your chances of success. It's all about finding out about the things that can trip you up and then avoiding them.

There are more than 120 Enterprise Agencies, so at least one will be close to where you live and work. They are independent, bringing together public and private sector money to fund what is often free of charge business advice.

Between them, Enterprise Agencies help some 20,000 business start-ups and 45,000 established businesses every year. If you are starting or growing a business, I would encourage you to do two things. First, visit *www.nfea.com* and make contact with your local Enterprise Agency. Second, buy this book, take it home and use it as an aide-memoire to success. Good luck!

Kevin Horne, Chairman, National Federation of Enterprise Agencies
www.nfea.com

Small Firms Enterprise Development Initiative

SFEDI is advised by all the major small business membership organisations and is run by small business owners for small business owners. SFEDI aims to find and promote the very best in business support and training to enable those starting up and running their own business to survive and thrive.

SFEDI chairman, Tony Robinson, says, 'This book is the very best. Once SFEDI found it, after Robert Ashton handed it to me, we endorsed it. Why? Because this is really valuable, entrepreneur-friendly, practical advice that works. It will help you to start and grow your business.'

Tony goes on to say, 'Many academics and government folk seem to think that us "would be" entrepreneurs are pretty thick and should find more time to meet with "their people" who know better than "wot we do". My advice is don't listen to anyone who hasn't got an "I run my own business" T-shirt. Robert has a wardrobe full of these T-shirts and you can smell it in every checklist. Enjoy.'

Tony Robinson, Chairman SFEDI *www.sfedi.co.uk*

1 Inspiration

generating your winning idea

10 ways to find time to plan

We're all busy people and finding time to plan your new enterprise can be a challenge. Remember that what you need to do at the outset is to think and you can do that almost anywhere. Here then are ten ways you can find the time to plan.

1. **Daydream** – something deep inside is urging you to consider setting up on your own. Stop reading right now, sit back, close your eyes, breathe deeply and imagine what your enterprise might look like.

2. **Ask your family** – parents, partners and even children have a knack of knowing us better than we think. What's more, if your parents have had their own business then, statistically, your own venture is more likely to succeed.

3. **Check your diary** – in the early days you won't have time for golf or nights in the pub. Cut back on your social life to plan your business. If it's too difficult, you might need to think again.

4. **Break a leg** – OK this is a bit drastic. Often though, it does take an enforced spell at home to really think things through. Why not take a sabbatical from work?

5. **Lose the phone** – try travelling with your mobile phone switched off, and use the freedom from distraction to explore your business ideas.

6. **Indulge your partner** – book that dream activity holiday and then while you sit in the bar reflecting, planning and thinking, your partner can be skiing, diving or climbing and warming to the idea!

7. **Walk the dog** – those early morning forays will test your fortitude, commitment and willingness to get out of bed on Sunday mornings. Fresh air is good for creative thinking.

8. **Ask the boss** – in today's enlightened workplace, leaving to start on your own can be viewed quite positively. If your boss rates you, they may well become your first client.

9. **Paint the house** – decorating will give you more time confined to one room, free of cerebral distraction. It might also mark, in a physical way, the start of a new way of life.

10. **Wallow** – instead of the hurried shower, soak in the bath and let your mind wander.

Businesses are started by people from all walks of life. We are all different and often create a business that focuses on meeting the needs of people like ourselves. Whatever your age, background, disability, education or sexual orientation, there's probably a business opportunity somewhere waiting for you to define it.

NEIL was a teacher working with special needs kids. He had a winter when he and his partner Will were both off with flu at the same time. As they recovered, they talked and realised that neither was particularly happy at work. Will had worked in the hospitality business at one time and they wondered about running a guest house in Cornwall.

When they felt better, they had their house valued and contacted some estate agents on the Cornish coast. They found they could afford to buy a five-bedroomed B&B and have some cash spare as working capital. As Neil said, 'If it wasn't for the flu, we might never have found time to talk properly and ... well, daydream about the business idea that has now become a reality.'

10 characteristics successful entrepreneurs often share

Starting and building a business is not easy. You need resilience, stamina and courage to get through the tough times we all experience. Here are ten characteristics to look for in yourself that many successful entrepreneurs share.

1. **Vision** – without a clear picture of what you want your life to look like, it will be difficult to create it. Successful entrepreneurs can see the detail as well as the big picture.

2. **Determination** – you want to do this don't you? Deal with any nagging doubts before you start. Determined people never turn back, but find ways round the inevitable obstacles.

3. **Fitness** – running your own business can be physically demanding. Keeping fit helps.

4. **Mental health** – starting a growing a business can be stressful. Don't be overambitious or put yourself under too much pressure. Know your limits and stay within them.

5. **Love** – you are going to need a shoulder to cry on, even if you're a man. If you've someone to share the thrills and spills with, you'll enjoy it more.

6. **Cash** – inevitably your business will take longer than you think to pay you a wage. Some businesses take years to turn in a profit. Make sure you are able to wait.

7. **Flexibility** – when most people start a business, they do it on their own. That means they have to do everything themselves – even unblock the drains!

8. **Humour** – you're going to make some mistakes – we all do. The ability to laugh it off, learn quickly and move on is what keeps really successful people going.

9. **Caution** – sometimes it's easy to see the opportunities and difficult to spot the threats. You need to be cautious, without being totally risk averse.

10. **Generosity** – when you enjoy success, invest in those who made it possible. Parties, thank-you gifts and nice surprises will keep everyone who matters on your side.

Many people dream of starting their own business when they've found the time to stop and think. However, most find the reality much harder to face. You need to be a special sort of person to work for yourself, perhaps even to employ others. As well as the strengths listed, you need a passion for the work you plan to do. Some are able to turn a hobby into a business. Turning a hobby into a business means you are doing something you know and like. Ideally it also needs to be capable of being scaled up and providing the income you are seeking.

Hobby businesses work best when:

- many people share your passion for . . . whatever;
- the specialist supplies or services you plan to provide are hard to find;
- there are dedicated enthusiast magazines or websites that reach your marketplace;
- you already have a good profile in the sector;
- interest is growing, not waning.

Good examples of hobby businesses include:

- bead shops that sell all you need to make costume jewellery;
- classical CD stores;
- model-making supplies;
- photographers.

STEVEN had always had a passion for photography and decided that he would like to turn professional. He knew it would be tough establishing himself and making a living in the north-east. Equally, he knew that he had real talent and could produce commercial work that people would pay for.

A grant and a loan from the Prince's Trust enabled Steven to rent a small studio in a recently developed 'artists' quarter' beside the river in Durham. This gave him a shop window and passing trade to boost his work and build his reputation. 'I'm young, keen and determined to succeed,' he told me, 'but getting help with rent for my studio has made it all possible.'

10 steps to generating your big idea

Whether you are simply too busy to think, feel that your brain is stagnating or are somewhere between the two extremes, generating the big idea is a daunting challenge. Here are ten ways to start the creative process.

1. **Buy a notebook** – keep it in your pocket, beside the bed and everywhere you go. Ideas can strike at any time. Write them down.

2. **Ask a friend** – who knows you well. Ask what they would buy from you, what you are good at and what they feel you should avoid.

3. **Beware of the hobby habit** – many people feel that their hobby holds the key, but are there enough people who share your passion and have money to spend?

4. **Watch the weather** – will your idea appeal to your customers all year round? Selling Christmas decorations or hiring bikes might not keep you in groceries for a full year. Perhaps you could run two seasonal businesses.

5. **Read books** – as well as reading this one, pick up some biographies of entrepreneurs you admire. See how they started, often in a small way, and then became household names. What can you learn from their experience and apply to your own situation?

6. **Open your eyes** – all around you are people running businesses. What do you think you could do better? You may not want to run a coffee shop, but thinking about how the one you visit every morning could improve will help you think more entrepreneurially.

7. **Stroll in the park** – and other places you only rarely visit. Watch people. What's missing? Observe, if possible, your potential customers. How can you influence them?

8. **Travel** – you don't need to go far. Visit local trade fairs and see what is promoted there. Pose as a buyer and ask questions. Compare your business vision with what you are experiencing.

9. **Check your CV** – most people actually start a business in an area in which they have worked before. Don't take this for granted, but accept it as a possibility all the same.

10. **Shake the pig** – emptying your money box onto the bed is the ultimate reality check for the budding entrepreneur. If Auntie Violet has just died

and left you a million, your choice is wide. For most of us though, cash will constrain our start-up plans.

Every business you can think of was started as a result of someone's inspiration. The initial idea will have been prompted by many inspirational factors. Unless you have been in business before, each good idea you generate will prompt a doubt. The battle for supremacy between inspiration and doubt creates the tension that urges exploration. Only the foolhardy start a business without considering the downside as well as the opportunity.

MARK

Newly married with a young baby, Mark had recently moved house and was annoyed that some of their treasured wedding presents had been damaged in transit. 'We hired a van and moved ourselves, packing our stuff in boxes we'd saved up from the supermarket. Some stuff got crushed when I had to brake sharply and that really upset my wife.'

The next week, buying shelves for their new home in a DIY store, Mark spotted piles of plastic crates. 'I wish we'd had those when we moved,' said his wife. That innocent remark got Mark thinking and resulted in him setting up, with his friend Jonathan, a business that hires out plastic crates to people moving house. Van hire companies and estate agents passed on his leaflets and the new business was born.

Part-time or full-time?

There are strong arguments both for and against starting your business part-time. On the one hand you are reducing your risk by starting in a modest way, and on the other you are limiting your chance of success by spreading yourself too thinly.

Here are some points you might consider.

Full-time	Part-time
More time to work on your business	Less need to earn from the business
Always there for customers	A danger of missing opportunities
Big commitment	Can encourage complacency
Might look foolhardy	Might look risk averse

10 things to check before chucking your job

Before you throw away a promising career to start up on your own, it's good to pause and take an objective look at the job you might be about to leave.

Five things that might make you stay at work

1. **I can buy out when the boss retires** – so will end up with my own business anyway.

2. **I've a life-threatening condition and the company will be generous** – although illness can give you a 'happy go lucky' approach, it may be best to seek fulfilment in your home life rather than become an entrepreneur.

3. **I qualify for a bumper pension in two years** – so why not hold fire and try to negotiate an early release? It'll be easier to start a business if you're receiving a pension.

4. **I actually like work, but my partner is pushing me** – is an all too common comment made by reluctant entrepreneurs. Should your partner start the business instead?

5. **They're currently funding my MBA** – which means that a start-up venture has never looked so appealing. Write the plan but wait until you get the piece of paper before resigning. Is there an opportunity to start a joint venture with your employer?

Five things that might make you decide to leave

1. **The boss is a control freak who'll never let go** – if work is uncomfortable and you think you can do better on your own, it's often worth giving it a go.

2. **I think the firm's going down the tube** – ask if it's true. If it is, you might be able to buy the assets from the receiver and get off to a flying start with the business you know.

3. **I have a personal pension scheme** – so however old you are you won't lose out financially when you're old.

4. **Work is depressing me** – life really is too short to spend it doing something you don't enjoy. Understand what it is about work that you want to change first though.

5. **I've been trading on the side and am getting busier** – many businesses start because moonlighting is proving successful. Make sure you're not breaching your employment contract.

It's all too easy to decide that work is the cause of your unhappiness and that all will be well if you start out on your own. As with almost everything in life though, you can reduce the risk and dip your toe in the water by going part-time at work. This gives you time to try out your business idea without cutting yourself off completely from the security of regular income.

Going part-time helps you test the water

Full-time	Part-time
You can grow faster	You'll grow more slowly
Need to make money sooner	You keep a salary as the business builds
More stressful, it feels 'all or nothing'	Also stressful, juggling too many balls
Always able to respond to customers	Have to fit customers around work
People will take you seriously	People may not take you seriously

Of course, management gurus such as Charles Handy have long advocated the 'portfolio career', where you build a collection of earning activities that suit your skills, lifestyle and income aspirations. For some, therefore, starting a new business part-time, while perhaps going part time at work, is the best way forward.

SIMON

An experienced project manager with 20 years' public sector experience, Simon did an MBA and found it a life-changing experience. 'It filled in the gaps in my knowledge and I developed a real interest in marketing. I wanted to have a go on my own, but with three kids at school didn't dare to risk giving up my salary at County Hall.'

His MBA group introduced him to people in other organisations willing to pay for Simon's expertise. He negotiated a deal that allowed him to work three days a week for the council and spend two days each week developing his own business. Within three months, however, he found he was turning away work and realised that he could not sit on the fence for long. He resigned and took the plunge. 'It was too easy to cling to what I knew,' he said, 'and in reality I was too cautious. Now I'm working full-time in my business I've never been happier.'

2 Goals

matching the idea to your personal aspiration

10 questions to ask yourself as you start to plan

Only you know what the important things are in your life. Starting a business is a great way to realise ambitions and achieve goals. You need to make sure that running a business is what you really want to do, and not simply something someone close to you is suggesting. Ask yourself these questions.

1. **What turns you on?** – this business is going to dominate your life for several years. You need to find the work you'll be doing exciting and stimulating, not dull.

2. **How rich do you want to be?** – how wealthy do you want to become and why? Perhaps you aspire to more than just money?

3. **What would you do if you could afford to?** – what are the world issues you'd like to change? If you make a mint, maybe you could invest in changing the world!

4. **Is your family behind you?** – your business must fit with their plans too. Remember that your partner as well as you may have to make sacrifices. Make sure they're with you.

5. **What do you want for your kids?** – watch them sleeping. What do you want for their future? How will your business deliver it?

6. **'Take a risk' rating** – ask yourself if you are really a risk taker or if borrowing money would keep you awake at night. Maybe a slow, steady start is better than a debt-laden big bang?

7. **What are the things that really matter to you?** – have you ever sat quietly in a place of worship watching the comings and goings? Make time to go somewhere spiritual and reflect on your personal values, priorities and goals.

8. **Where does it fit in the big picture?** – take a long walk and watch nature. It's a great way to put your new venture in perspective with the world.

9. **Who are your business heroes?** – read how some of your business heroes got started. Remember, every big successful business was once small and fragile.

10. **What use are notes?** – you are embarking on an exciting journey which, one day, others will want to learn about. Keep a diary and record your feelings.

Of course, as Douglas Adams said in *The Hitchhiker's Guide to the Galaxy*, the answer to the ultimate question is 42. For you and me it is probably a little more complex and you will find that the more you achieve then the higher your aspiration will become. This is the phenomenon defined by Maslov as his 'hierarchy of needs':

- physiological – food, water, sleep, sex;
- safety – freedom from physical harm;
- social – friendship, a feeling of belonging;
- ego – respect and status;
- self-actualisation – developing talents and realising potential.

Maslov argued that we can move up and down the list as our fortunes flourish or falter, but our ambition will always be to seek self-actualisation.

SIMONE was born in Rwanda and had a daughter. Life was tough with civil war, poverty and hunger destroying her country. She wanted her daughter to have an education and a future. They managed to escape to England and applied for asylum. She learned to speak English and trained to be a hairdresser, but finding work as a refugee was difficult.

The Prince's Trust gave her a grant and a mentor which enabled her to open her own salon in an upmarket gym. Now she has her own business specialising in African hairstyles. Her daughter attends the local school. Simone's determination to escape and start afresh gave her the courage to start her business.

10 ways to involve your family in your dream

Small businesses can be more demanding than small children. It makes sense to get the whole family involved in your new venture. If nothing else, it will stop them turning into strangers as you battle away on your own.

1. **Search the net** – let's face it, your kids are probably better at finding stuff online than you are. Why not get them to research your idea?

2. **Mystery shopping** – once you've spotted who your rivals are, get your relatives to contact them posing as potential customers. Recognise that others might do this to you!

3. **Visit the bank** – if your partner does your banking, perhaps in their lunch hour, they will see how well your business is doing. It also saves you having to go.

4. **Insource** – when you start out, managing costs is almost as important as generating sales. Use family labour to carry out the tasks you will one day outsource – stuffing envelopes, packing consignments, etc.

5. **Carry the phone** – if you're out of the (home) office a lot and your partner is at home with the kids, a portable phone will be useful for taking messages for you. Make sure the baby doesn't cry!

6. **Paint the walls** – starting a business is fun. Have the whole family help you prepare your office, shop or workshop.

7. **Fill the vase** – if you're a man you'll probably overlook some of the things that a woman would remember. Ask your partner to be responsible for keeping some flowers on your desk – it'll brighten your day.

8. **Change the fuse** – alternatively, if you're a woman, however competent at DIY, your partner will probably welcome being invited to be your maintenance man.

9. **Book a break** – you're busy and working hard but you need to take time out from time to time. Set some dates, discuss a budget and have your partner surprise you and book regular breaks – even an evening out is often enough.

10. **Buy the vision** – everyone close to you needs to appreciate your vision for the enterprise you're establishing. It will make the inevitable sacrifices seem worthwhile.

Many people will tell you that you should never start a business with family or close friends. This is because emotional ties can make it difficult to remain objective and,

as many family firms have found, it's difficult to fire someone you live with! However, many of the most successful businesses are run by husband and wife, brother and sister or long-term friends. You simply have to make sure that you put the business need first, rather than simply create a role for someone you love.

Protect your relationship if you work with family or friends

- Have a written partnership or shareholder agreement that defines the deal.
- Use written job descriptions to define roles and job boundaries.
- Avoid intimacy in the workplace.
- Don't show favour – treat everyone the same.
- If you work with your partner, don't discuss work at home – have a life outside!

MALCOLM & MALCOLM

Best friends at college, the two Malcolms decided they'd like to set up a business together when they graduated. Both fascinated by IT, they established a software business and later moved into internet services. Outside work, they have quite different interests and rarely meet socially. 'We knew we could trust each other and shared similar values when it came to the basics of running a business,' they told me.

After more than 25 years, they are still working together and still happy. Their roles have evolved over the years as their business has grown. When it comes to making decisions though, they always share responsibility.

10 common worries and how to overcome them

It's natural to have attacks of self-doubt. Starting a business is a big responsibility and you're very much on your own. Here are ten common worries and how to overcome them.

1. **I'm not bright enough** – well, sometimes you can be too bright to succeed. Innocence and naivety can actually protect you from fear. It is possible to think too much!

2. **I'm not pushy enough** – do you like doing business with pushy people or do you prefer nice reasonable people? Pushy people are often less successful than you might think.

3. **I'm not rich enough** – one of the best ways to watch your costs is to have no money to waste. Wealthy people can be careless with money – you probably can't afford to be.

4. **I'm not good at sums** – relax, spreadsheets and accounting software make the numbers easy to work out. Remember that success is as much about instinct as arithmetic.

5. **I can't spell** – literacy is great if you want to write books but less important if your business communicates with customers verbally. Use document templates – there are some at the back of this book.

6. **I'll fail** – maybe you will, but equally you won't make your first million if you don't try.

7. **Rivals will eat me alive** – in fact the opposite is usually the case. Young, small businesses can duck and weave beneath the fists of those nasty big competitors.

8. **I'm naturally pessimistic** – so, you won't make false assumptions and step into the dark without a torch, will you! A glance at the downside puts the upside in perspective – just be sure to see both.

9. **I don't take risks** – running a business is like crossing the road. You can jaywalk, wear dark clothing and risk getting squashed – or push the button and follow the green man when the traffic stops. There's almost always a choice.

10. **I know my failings** – we all know what we're bad at and we all underestimate the value of our strengths. No one is perfect and nor is any business. That's why there's room for you too. Focus on what you do well.

Self-confidence is the product of knowledge and experience. Rather like riding a bike, playing a musical instrument or even making love, the more you practise the better you'll get.

Try to be objective and see through the marketing hype rivals might be spreading around. Every entrepreneur has doubts, second thoughts and fears – you're not alone.

ADRIAN

After completing a music degree, in which he developed his passion for piano and classical guitar, Adrian looked for a career. Lacking the confidence to set up as a full-time teacher, he got a job washing dishes in a pizza restaurant. In his spare time he played in local bands. After a while, when the daily grind of washing dishes was beginning to get him down but a better job had still not been found, a friend dared him to go it alone. His local Enterprise Agency provided free business training and also found him a mentor with whom he could share his moments of doubt.

After 15 months Adrian had hung up his apron and rubber gloves and found enough pupils to pay his bills and enable him to devote his whole life to the music he loves. As he will readily admit, 'I was the only person holding me back; once I'd found the confidence to try, it was much easier to set up my business than I thought.'

10 ways that every entrepreneur is different

Not everyone wants to make a million – many simply want to spend time doing what they love. It's rarely black or white, but here are some opposites that will help you think where you sit between them.

1. **Rich or poor?** – if your household income doubled, what would you do differently? For some people, sudden wealth erodes personal values and brings misery. How much more would make you happy?

2. **Indoors or outdoors?** – do you like fresh air? If so, pay someone else to do the office work and spend your time out and about doing something you enjoy.

3. **Home or away?** – travelling to far flung destinations is an enjoyable part of business life for some people. Others prefer to sleep in their own bed every night. Do you want to travel, or can you find the business you need close to home?

4. **Head or hands?** – thinking suits some people, craftsmanship others. You must choose how your time will be spent. As a craft business grows, its founder often leaves the workshop for the office but this need not be the case. You make the rules.

5. **Night or day?** – are you a lark or an owl? Few newsagents or bakers dislike early mornings and you won't find an early bird running a night club. Match your enterprise to your body's natural rhythms.

6. **Alone or in a crowd?** – gregarious people like to work with people, others are more reclusive. Which are you?

7. **Fast or slow?** – some business people thrive on short deadlines, surprise orders and multitasking (for example, distribution). Others prefer a more sedate style of work where time to reflect and think is valued (for example, law).

8. **Dirty or clean?** – like little boys and puddles, some entrepreneurs love cleaning blocked drains or rendering abattoir waste. Others prefer to import and distribute scented candles and incense sticks from mystical places.

9. **Healthy or harmful?** – selling cigarettes, guns or booze gives some people a problem. If you're not comfy making money through encouraging people

to damage their health, or that of others, leave nasty products to others. Only do what you feel comfortable with.

10. **Fat or thin?** – believe it or not, some businesses strike most of their deals over large lunches and dinners. If you're a closet gourmet you will relish the opportunity to munch your way to success. If you're a weightwatcher this will be less attractive.

One of the major problems encountered by a growing business is that the founder gets to spend less time doing enjoyable things and more time in the office. This usually kicks in when you need to employ more than five people to handle the workload. The trouble is that it's almost always easier and cheaper to hire someone to do what you used to do than to find someone capable of managing the paperwork. Crossing this barrier is often too great a problem and many owner-managers (often subconsciously) keep their business small enough to enable them to do the things they enjoy. Business advisers sometimes scathingly refer to these as 'lifestyle businesses'. There's nothing wrong with running a lifestyle business – it's your life after all. If, however, you do want to grow there are ways in which you can structure your business so that you do not lose touch with the coalface.

ROB has had a varied and interesting career but a few years ago decided that he gained the most satisfaction from mending roofs. With his children having left home and the mortgage just about paid off, he didn't need a huge income to lead the sort of life he and his wife envisaged. They also wanted to be able to take weeks off at a time to travel and explore all the places they'd read about over the years. To have this degree of freedom, Rob knew that he would need his business to be either very small or large enough to afford a manager who could lead the team when he was away.

The deciding factor was that his children both had good jobs and he didn't feel a need to build up an inheritance for their old age. Now, with Rick, his young assistant, Rob mends roofs for people living within an easy drive of his home. He regularly turns work away, choosing to do just enough to fund the lifestyle he has chosen to lead. Rob is one of the happiest entrepreneurs you could ever meet.

3 Knowledge

researching your idea/reality checking

10 ways to research on the internet

There is almost too much information out there to sift through when planning to attack a new market or start a new venture. You need to be selective and focused. It should rarely be necessary to buy data. Here are ten top research tips.

1. **Google** – everyone uses search engines and Google is the most popular. However, try the 'advanced search' facility which enables you to use more search criteria to improve the quality of what comes back.

2. **Check rivals** – look at the sites of those you compete with. Register to receive their regular newsletter or RSS feed – let them tell you what they're up to!

3. **Search people** – research the people you want to do business with, or who perhaps compete with you. Find out what they're involved with – read their blogs, read criticism and praise.

4. **Read minutes** – most public organisations publish meeting minutes on the web. This can give you valuable background information if you're tendering for public sector work.

5. **Learn search techniques** – there are some clever things you can do with '&' and other symbols to gain specific information. Some examples are listed opposite.

6. **Ask the obvious** – if you want to know what a word means, type into the search engine the phrase 'xxxxx means' and you'll probably get a definition back.

7. **Join a newsgroup** – these are popular at home as well as at work. News and user groups give you access to a community of people most likely to know the answers to your questions. Ask people as well as a search engine.

8. **Numbers count** – many people forget that search engines can search phone numbers and postcodes. Google your own work phone number – you may be surprised what is revealed!

9. **Go to university** – you'll be amazed at how much new knowledge you can harvest from a university's website. Find the homepages of the academics researching your business sector. Most will have hyperlinks to papers they've written. Also visit university library sites – they're full of free information.

10. **Check out books** – the book reviews on sites such as Amazon often contain enough to inform you without having to buy the book.

Internet search techniques

Now that you've considered what you want to find, you want to get to the right pages quickly without having to scroll through endless near misses. Search engines are, of course, nothing more than computer programs – you need to tell them exactly what you are looking for in a way that their code understands. Here are some techniques gleaned from a variety of sources that you will find useful. Copy this page and keep it by your computer.

- **Use the best word** – avoid common words and use those that closely match what you are seeking. Enclosing words in inverted commas asks the engine to find those words in that order. So '80 gsm copier paper' will find suppliers of copier paper of that weight, whereas searching for 'copier paper', or worse 'paper', will deliver many unwanted results. You also need to try to use the words that the person who built the site might have anticipated would be search words.

- **Boolean logic** – is a techie phrase for something quite simple. It uses the words AND, OR and NOT to filter results and present you with what you want. For example:
  - *locksmith* AND *Epping* will exclude locksmiths based elsewhere;
  - *new cars* AND *Epping* NOT *Ford* will exclude Ford dealers but show you the rest;
  - *new cars* AND *Epping Ford* OR *Vauxhall* will give you only dealers selling Ford or Vauxhall cars.

  You can also use + or & for AND, and – for NOT.

- **Capitals** – search engines are not case sensitive so you don't need to worry about capitals or lower case letters.

- **Parts of words** – some search engines will automatically search for and include variations of the words you search for. An example is 'dietary' which will also return pages showing diet.

10 good questions to ask yourself and others

All too often, the experts we ask for advice overlook some of the most obvious ways of researching a new market. It doesn't matter if you're planning a new business or looking to enter a new market. Here are ten questions many people forget to ask.

1. **Would you buy it?** – if you're selling to people like you, ask yourself if you'd pay the price and keep coming back for more. If not, why not?

2. **Would they buy it?** – obvious and simple, but so many try to guess what the customer would say. Ask some prospective customers and hear it straight from the horse's mouth.

3. **Who already does it?** – check trade and online directories to see who's already offering what you're planning to offer. How can you be different?

4. **Where is it done best?** – take a journey to see the largest, fastest, best players in the business sector you're exploring. Few people travel to research their new ideas, so what you find works elsewhere may work for you at home.

5. **Does no competitors mean no market?** – there is very little that's completely new. Usually it's best to let someone else do the pioneering stuff, and then you can do it better. Worry if you seem to be the first – there may be no market demand.

6. **Would you be my mystery shopper?** – ask some friends to pose as customers and contact your rivals. Their feedback will reveal a lot about your competition and help you make your business different.

7. **Can you spare me five minutes?** – ask potential customers if they'd mind answering some questions about what they expect from a supplier. You're not selling, you're gathering information. It's to their benefit to cooperate so many will agree to talk.

8. **Why is nobody selling XYZ here?** – find businesses selling to your target market and ask them why no one's tried what you're planning to do. Has someone had a go and failed? Find out why and make sure you don't repeat their mistakes.

9. **Why have you no outlets here?** – ask your suppliers why no one in your area has distributed their product before. Get their marketing people researching your idea – they will benefit from your success too.

10. **Does this feel right to me?** – finally listen to your inner voice or instinct. Does this business idea feel right? Make sure you're not simply trying to convince yourself.

It is almost as easy to do too much research as too little. The most successful entrepreneurs rely as much on instinct and hunch as they do on research. If it feels right they do it anyway. Remember that many of the world's most widely used products and services were established on a hunch or by chance. The computer, the telephone and the motor car were all initially reckoned to have little long-term potential.

As an entrepreneur you have to balance your instinct against what you hear from those around you. The key to success, or even survival, is to manage risk and minimise the impact of failure. If you try different strategies some will fail as surely as others will succeed. Rather like the professional gambler, you need to have your stake money put aside and risk only that in testing your new market.

RUPERT

A successful retailer of pine furniture and accessories with three outlets, Rupert wanted to expand his business. Most pine furniture is sold by large retailers, with smaller market towns often being the best place for independent outlets. He narrowed his choice to three towns:

- Woodbridge – small, coastal, affluent;
- Bury St Edmunds – large, fairly affluent, close to many people;
- Colchester – very large, several retail parks, diverse.

He paid someone to research each town and gathered lots of statistics from retail units, the local authority and list brokers and so could build a profile of the population. He also paid someone to visit each town and talk to retailers.

Which town did he choose? Well actually, he chose to stick with the three outlets he had and to encourage people to come to him from further away. He realised that he had a fourth option – to invest the cash in better marketing for his existing outlets. Entrepreneurs often change their minds for all the right reasons.

10 people who might do your research for free

You can spend too much time researching. Here are ten ways you can encourage people to do the hard work for you.

1. **Advertising rep** – find the journals that reach your market and ask their advertising people why they deliver value. They will usually provide you with statistics from their research, and may even tell you about your rivals' advertising success.

2. **List broker** – you can buy lists of just about every type of person, business or organisation. A broker will tell you how many prospects there are. You don't have to buy the list!

3. **Government** – you'd be amazed how much data is posted on the internet by Government departments and agencies. Ring the helpline and sweet-talk someone into extracting the data for you.

4. **Students** – college and school staff need business studies projects. If your research involves a lot of legwork, use students' legs to cover the ground.

5. **Trade associations** – you may not have joined the trade body that represents the sector you're exploring, but ring the librarian or information officer and ask for a membership list. Their website may well contain many useful downloads that will help you.

6. **Quangos** – most quangos publish weighty documents that show why they are needed and what they seek to do. If a quango exists to support your audience, ask to be sent whatever is available.

7. **Suppliers** – if you are a distributor, potential suppliers will usually be more than happy to let you have market information. They will already have researched it.

8. **Customers** – if the customer wants you to do something new, suggest it will happen faster if they can find others who will also buy. It's cheaper then for everyone.

9. **Undergraduates** – most universities have a website that markets work opportunities to students. Often, you can recruit a student to do your research for little more than the minimum wage. Many welcome an alternative to serving fast food to make money.

10. **Volunteers** – charities use volunteers all the time for fund-raising and much more. Sometimes you can recruit volunteers, or perhaps people with special needs, to assemble and collate market surveys in exchange for an appropriate donation to their cause.

Sometimes, the answer is right under your nose and you do not need to look very far at all to find the researcher you need.

> **COLETTE**
>
> Passionate about crafts, Colette wanted to set up an internet business that would make it easier to sell her work, as well as the work of others. Being a wheelchair user, getting out researching her business was not easy. 'Everything takes much longer and I need specialist office equipment so I cannot easily work in libraries.'
>
> Fortunately, her son needed to write a business plan as part of his advanced business studies course. Colette suggested her own business idea for this project and so her son did all the research and applied the techniques his course had taught him to prepare a plan that worked for them both. He passed his course and Colette started her business.

Entrepreneurship and disability

It would have been easy for Colette to give up. Severe arthritis means that she really needs to work from home so that she can work when her condition allows and rest when necessary. She needed specialist seating and office furniture, together with an ergonomic computer keyboard and mouse. As her own employer, she was able to obtain a Government grant of several thousand pounds to cover the cost of equipment. If you have a physical condition that makes starting or operating your business a real challenge, you may also qualify for help towards the cost of the things you need.

10 steps to convincing yourself your idea will work

Before writing your business plan you need to check that you're on the right track. This is the right time to turn back if you have nagging doubts. Here's a final ten-step, pre-start-up checklist to help you decide if your idea really is going to work.

1. **Will it last?** – a business is like a dog, it will demand your attention several times a day until you sell it or it dies. It has to excite you or you will not find the energy to succeed.

2. **Will my partner approve?** – a business cannot be cited as the 'other party' in a divorce, your life partners may become jealous of your new passion. Make sure yours won't.

3. **Does mum like it?** – parents like to be consulted, it makes them feel wanted. Remember that if they approve of your enterprise they may be able to help in some way.

4. **Deep pockets?** – are you going to run out of cash before the business gets off the ground? Before you read about business plans, listen to your instinct.

5. **What does bad look like?** – we all have different pain barriers and it's good to imagine what apocalypse looks like to you. Are you hooked on the good things in life or are you prepared to put it all on the line?

6. **Fallback skills?** – don't get too depressed, but if the proverbial hits the fan how would you earn a crust? Everyone has baseline skills (driving, cooking, selling, etc.). Imagine doing it for a living. That is your worse-case scenario.

7. **What exactly do you want to achieve?** – ask yourself again if it's money that motivates you. Do you want to change lives? You may be happier starting a social enterprise.

8. **Are you a self-starter?** – you're going to experience ups and downs. Have you the resilience to bounce back when someone or something's knocked you for six?

9. **Do you like surprises?** – the entrepreneur who doesn't get surprised lives with their eyes closed. If you want an orderly, predictable life don't start or buy a business.

10. **Read Kipling** – take a moment to look up that famous poem 'If'. If you can read the poem and see yourself having the strength to succeed – read on!

Sometimes, however, the urge to just 'go for it' is too strong to resist and you'll ignore the so-called warning signs and do it anyway. The key point to remember is to limit your risk so that if it doesn't work out, you can survive to try again another day.

BRIAN

An artist himself, Brian wanted to start an art publishing business that would make it easier for artists and buyers to connect. A modest inheritance gave him the capital he needed and he opened a small gallery and framing shop in an affluent town close to the Cotswolds.

One year on, he is running out of cash and the business has not taken off as quickly as he had hoped. He says he has found out a lot about entrepreneurship and, while he has no regrets, wishes he had known at the outset what he knows now. His experience has made him even more determined to succeed and he is working with his local Business Link to focus the business.

He has invested his aunt's legacy in a year of learning that has probably taught him as much (and cost about the same) as a full-time MBA. Now, he is planning to raise the capital to create and market a virtual gallery, which will supplement his actual gallery. Brian considered the risks and decided to do it anyway. Some might call him foolhardy but, informed by his recent experiences, he is now poised to take the corporate art market by storm. Would an MBA have prepared him as well for the successful future he now faces?

4 Business plan

convincing yourself and others

10 things every business plan should contain

Every enterprise should have a business plan. It does not need to be lengthy or filled with jargon. Focus instead on making it short, simple, specific and, above all else, realistic. Remember that an overambitious business plan may fool others, but you're the fool left holding the can if it doesn't work out. Here are ten things your plan should contain.

1. **Vision** – capture in a sentence what is it that makes this business exciting and utterly irresistible to customers, suppliers and, most importantly, to you.

2. **Background** – describe how you came to conclude that this is the right business to be in right now. What are the circumstances that are coinciding to create your opportunity?

3. **Goals** – what are the specific short, medium and long-term goals by which success will be measured?

4. **People** – who is in your team and how are they perfect for the job?

5. **Products/services** – what are you going to sell and what are the main benefits they offer over what you know is available elsewhere?

6. **Competition** – who's already out there and how will you be different? The differences are crucially important – without knowing them you will not succeed.

7. **Marketing** – how are you going to communicate the benefits you offer to those you seek as customers? How will you measure the response and improve marketing effectiveness?

8. **Funding** – how will you pay for it all and what can investors (if any) expect in return?

9. **Risk** – show that you've assessed the risks to your success and have them covered.

10. **Jumping ship** – a business, like anything else, has a natural lifespan. You need to plan for your exit before you start. Will you sell? Give it to your kids? What?

It is no coincidence that this checklist is one of the shortest in the book. The biggest mistake people make when writing a business plan is to make it too long because then no one reads it. Good business plans are:

- **concise** – to the point and focused;

- **emotional** – you want to do this like it hurts so tell the reader why;

- **logical** – giving you and any reader confidence;

- **factual** – demonstrating your understanding of the opportunity;

- **realistic** – not committing yourself to too much.

Every agency or bank that works with businesses will tell you that preparing the business plan is the essential first step. However, they will probably also tell you, if you ask them, that most business plans are filed in a drawer and never again looked at by those running the enterprise. The plan you write needs to be so relevant and useful that it becomes *part* of your business management. Here are a few myths about business plans.

- **I know my business and only need a plan to keep the bank happy** – sharing a simple, concise business plan with key employees is one of the best ways to keep their efforts aligned with your vision. Business plans are for you, not the bank.

- **Banks need lots of detail to show that you've considered all possible eventualities** – bank managers are people first and financiers second. The decision to lend will be made intuitively, with the manager's gut feeling for your business backed up by the plan you write. Bank managers see many plans so keep yours short.

- **I've downloaded a great business plan model from the internet** – the internet is full of business plan frameworks into which you can drop your business. However, it's often best to copy the headings and write your own plan, using only those headings that are relevant and ignoring those that are not.

- **A consultant wrote my plan and the bank lent me £50,000** – sometimes, consultants and accountants are the best people to write your pitch to a funder. However, their starting point should be a business plan that *you* have written. No one else can really get into your mind and put your passion into the plan.

10 things bank managers look for

Like it or not, unless you are already wealthy, you will need to borrow money. In fact building a business takes investment – it's not just when you start that you need to seek funds. Later, I cover where to look for funding but having to convince a bank manager to support you in some way is almost inevitable. Here are ten words that will impress.

1. **Vision** – yes, you must show that you have a clear vision and know just where you are heading. Your plan must paint a clear picture of your vision.

2. **Commitment** – however much money you plan to invest yourself, it will be expected that it will be enough to really hurt if the business fails and you lose it.

3. **Security** – as if commitment is not enough, banks usually want guarantees. This often means giving them a legal charge over your home or other assets.

4. **Cover** – how big is the risk you're taking? If you appear foolhardy, you'll get no support. The more success you have behind you the more popular you'll be.

5. **Market** – it helps if your banker understands your market. In some high-tech or biotech sectors, or in agriculture, it is usually best to seek out specialist bankers familiar with the vagaries of your sector.

6. **Skills** – your CV, and those of your key people, must read well. No bank will lend if your motive for starting is that you were sacked for failing in someone else's business.

7. **Health** – you need resilience and stamina. Invest in a medical check-up and add the report to your plan.

8. **Love** – the clever banker visits you at home to assess how committed your family is. Remember, it's often their home you're risking.

9. **Guts** – if you're too soft you won't chase your debts and might fall behind with loan repayments. You need to come over as tough, but not macho!

10. **Persuasiveness** – the ability to sell is the greatest asset in any entrepreneur. Don't appear too glib or too clever. Practise selling on the bank. You don't have to take all that's offered to you!

More stuff about banks

Everybody likes to knock banks. The fact is though that every business needs the services of a bank and, managed correctly, banks are an asset and not a threat to your success. Online banking is very convenient and gives you the comfort of being able to check at any time of the day or night that your customers have paid.

Banks are, however, a supplier to your business like any other and you should never be afraid to consider changing to another. Here's a checklist to help decide if your bank is giving you good service.

- Check out alternative banks if:
  - you find it difficult to get on with your bank manager;
  - the charge over your home is not relinquished, even if your business becomes a lower risk;
  - good-quality online banking is not available;
  - every meeting turns into a sales pitch for overpriced insurance products;
  - your bank seems not to understand your industry.

- You can make it easier to deal with your bank if you:
  - tell your bank manager (almost) everything and don't hold back information;
  - invite your bank manager to visit your business for a first-hand inspection;
  - discuss business over lunch or even in a convenient coffee house;
  - take a genuine interest in your bank manager as a person;
  - thank the bank for doing well, in addition to moaning when it goes wrong.

- Cash transactions – surprisingly, some banks do not like handling large amounts of coinage. Some work through the Post Office network and do not charge to take cash deposits.

- Credit cards – shop around before accepting your usual bank's 'merchant services' offer if you want to take credit cards. This is especially true if you plan to take online payments where there are specialist service providers.

10 figures you need to work out

Too many people keep working away in their business and never quite work out why the bank balance seems to hover at the overdraft limit permanently. The answer is to keep an eye on some important figures and ratios. Here are ten finance figures it's good to understand.

1. **Overheads** – the fixed costs of operating your business. The more you sell, the smaller your overhead costs proportionately become. If sales fall then overheads can cripple you.

2. **Variable costs** – incurred only when you produce something, for example raw materials. These costs are good because they are directly proportional to your sales.

3. **Profit** – as a rule of thumb, profit is the value of your sale less the associated variable costs less a proportion of your overhead costs. Many forget to include overhead costs in their costings and consequently lose money.

4. **Debtor days** – the average length of time customers make you wait for your money. As your business grows it becomes vital to keep this figure low.

5. **VAT** – if your sales rise above a certain level you have to add VAT. Most businesses then pay this on to HMRC quarterly. VAT sitting in your bank account can lead you think you've got more money to spend than you actually have. Take note!

6. **Creditor days** – the average length of time you string your suppliers along before paying your bills. Smart operators always pay the most important dependent suppliers first.

7. **Credit rating** – if you habitually pay your bills late and have perhaps had the odd court judgment made against your business, then your credit rating will be poor and people may ask for cash up front. Specialist agencies provide credit rating reports for a fee.

8. **Quick ratio** – is the easiest accounting ratio to watch and also the most important. It is the total of the debt owed you plus the cash in your bank, divided by the amount you owe creditors. So, if your debtors owe you £10,000 and your bank account stands at −£2000, and you owe creditors £4,000, your quick ratio is (£10,000–£2,000)/£4000 = 2. Above 1 and you are solvent, below 1 and you are not!

9. **Cash flow** – use a spreadsheet to calculate why you need your income to be phased to meet your predicted outgoings. Calculate the effect of people paying you late – it's alarming!

10. **Balance sheet and profit & loss** – these are reports that your accounting software will produce. Always look at the year-to-date figure as well as the last month's performance. You can rarely judge success on the strength of one month alone.

Figures people

The good news is that you do not have to do all the work yourself. Accounting software takes much of the hard work out of bookkeeping and there are people who specialise in keeping books for others. Five reasons for using a good book-keeper are:

- someone else is checking your figures;

- invoicing is not delayed because you are too busy;

- they save you time and hassle;

- accountant's bills are lower if a bookkeeper has done the basics;

- you have someone else who can chase overdue payments.

KATHRINE enjoys keeping accounts and wanted to combine working with starting a family. Networking with local businesses soon led to introductions to people who needed help with their accounts, and she was also advised by her local Enterprise Agency. She visits her clients every week but does most of the work on her computer at home.

She now has two children and an established portfolio of clients. Each of them values what she does for them and each is happy for her to collect paperwork and work at home. She plans her workload around her clients and her family. One day she may build the business, but for now she is enjoying the flexibility her business allows her.

10 pertinent points about business structure

Your financial adviser may advise you to structure your business solely to reduce tax. There are other equally important things to take into account. Here are ten of them.

1. **Risk** – if your business operates in fields where financial risks are high, it will be better to protect yourself by setting up a 'limited liability' company. This literally limits your personal liability, unless you can be proved to have acted wrongfully.

2. **Reward** – how much money do you expect, or want, to make? If your business is going to remain modest, it may be better to simply be self-employed.

3. **People** – shared ownership of a business can be very tax efficient. Equally, giving shares to people not involved from day to day (for example, your family) can be a problem if the relationship sours. Sometimes it's best to own the business outright and pay more tax!

4. **For sale?** – limited companies, because their accounting is reported to Companies House, are easier to sell because trading is more transparent.

5. **Socially motivated?** – if you are establishing a UK social enterprise, you might set up as a 'Community Interest Company'. This gives you the flexibility of a limited company and the transparency of purpose of a charity.

6. **Don't divorce** – not a pleasant thought, but if you put half of your business in your partner's name to save tax you'll have a problem if you separate.

7. **Selling up** – the tax treatment of the proceeds from the sale of business shares and assets often makes creating a company a good move. Take advice before you start.

8. **Customer perception** – in some marketplaces you are not taken seriously unless you have a limited company. This is perhaps rather silly but true all the same. You must decide if you are going to make a stand or follow the herd.

9. **Trading name** – even if you decide not to set up a limited company you can still use a memorable trading name. If the name you want is not registrable, you may still be able to be ABC Ltd, trading as Alphabets. One is the business and one the brand.

10. **Reputation** – just to remind you that what you do, and how others see your business, is actually more important than how you set the business up!

Some people go to extraordinary lengths to make their business appear to be something it isn't. This often has as much to do with their feelings of insecurity as any practical need. Here are some dos and don'ts about making your business look real.

- **You** – in most small businesses, like it or not, you are the business. How you behave, and indeed your level of confidence, will say most about the firm.

- **Phone** – answering the phone professionally, without background noises from children, the TV or your pet parrot, suggests you are in an office and focused on work.

- **Phone 2** – if you work from home invest in a separate business line. It's possible to forward calls and much more. Explore the options.

- **e-mail** – domain names are so cheap now that there really is no excuse for being *yourco@hotmail.com*. Buy your domain and look businesslike.

- **Address** – as long as you make sure that you use your postcode and talk nicely to your postman, you can drop '147 Station Road', and replace it with YourCo, Station Road.

RICHARD

A talented graphic designer and photographer, Richard couldn't afford to rent business premises when he started his business, preferring instead to invest in a top-of-the-range Apple Mac computer. He lived in a flat in a nice part of the city and decided to change his address to 'Studio 5, 123 The Street'. By calling his flat a studio and meeting his clients at their office, or in a convenient coffee shop, he saved money he would have spent in rent. He was also able to work when it suited him without having to leave home.

When his business had grown enough to employ an assistant, he did a deal with a client, moving into an empty office at their place and offsetting their work against the rent. This way, he also secured the long-term support of a key client.

10 things to include in a cash-flow forecast

Your business plan will inevitably contain forecasts and predictions. Certainly in the early days cash-flow forecasting is the most important factor as it will chart the journey to your financial goals. Checking your financial progress is vital if you are to stay on track. People often overlook or underestimate these ten aspects of finance.

1. **Cash** – always aim to borrow or invest more than the forecast says you need. This will allow for slippages later.

2. **Sales** – building up sales, be it a new business or a new product, always takes longer than you think. Be modest in the estimate for your early months.

3. **Purchases** – if you are to carry stock or use raw materials, it will take a while to reach to the right usage levels. Allow for overstocking at first.

4. **VAT** – many people forget to add VAT to purchases and sales, and to allow for the quarterly tax payment. VAT can both underpin and wreck cash flow!

5. **Employment costs** – as well as adding a percentage for National Insurance payments, you need to allow for staff training, temps for sickness cover and any equipment your staff will need. Use a payroll bureau to calculate your true employment costs.

6. **Paying the tax man** – it is foolhardy to delay paying the taxman. These HMRC officials may not shout loudly to start with but can turn very nasty very quickly.

7. **Marketing costs** – you will waste much of your marketing budget on experimenting. If sales are slow you may want to spend even more. Build 'more' into the forecast.

8. **Include options** – the above are all largely pessimistic points. Duplicate your forecast and add in some optimistic predictions. See how these make a huge impact on your need for cash. Now plan how to make some of those good things happen.

9. **Loan repayments** – at some point, you'll want your investment back, with interest. If it's the bank's money this will be prescribed. Include repayments in your forecast.

10. **Slippage** – work out what effect late payment by your customers will have on your cash requirement. Frightening, isn't it?

Microsoft Excel

Chances are you're pretty good at putting together spreadsheets. Just in case you're not, here are some top tips for MS Excel.

- A useful spreadsheet for calculating loan rates can be found under *General Templates > Spreadsheet Solutions > Loan Amortization.*

- Use the *Ctrl* and *:* keys together to enter the current date into a cell.

- Experiment with *Tools > Goal Seek*, especially with cash-flow forecasts. This can help in achieving desired profits by changing product/service rates.

- Remember that Excel has built-in database functionality. With long lists of data, try using *Data > Filter > AutoFilter* to add filtering options.

- Don't forget the Σ button on the standard toolbar. This can be used to sum ranges easily. Also, hidden in the dropdown menu are *Min*, *Max* and *Average* functions.

PAUL

After a career in health service accounting, Paul wanted to focus on both software training and work for himself. He knew, from his experience at work, that he was good at helping people build both confidence and skills with Microsoft products.

He took the plunge, rented a training room and purchased hardware and software. Most comfortable with small groups, he decided to make this a selling point. Business was slow to start with but after a lot of hard work and networking he found his diary starting to fill. Paul provided the Excel tips above.

5 Investment

how to fund start-up and growth

10 people who might invest in your business

Asking a bank for money is always a good starting point. They will check out your proposal for free and give you valuable feedback. However, the bank might not be your only option. Here are ten people you might ask to invest in your business.

1. **Yourself** – remember, the more you can invest yourself the more others will be inclined to put in. You can't expect others to invest in you if you choose not to.

2. **Your mortgage lender** – increasing the mortgage on the family home is the traditional and cheapest way to raise business capital. Be aware of the risk though.

3. **Parents** – be honest with them. You are probably a beneficiary of their will so all you are actually asking for is an advance. Check for tax benefits. Do not, however, jeopardise your family relationships.

4. **Siblings** – older brothers and sisters who are successful in their lives might be happy to invest in your success. Unlike parents, though, siblings will want a healthy return on their investment.

5. **Your boss** – you can negotiate a voluntary redundancy package. Alternatively, see if the firm will lend you the money – they might after all be your first customer.

6. **Your lover** – does your lover love you enough to lend you the cash? Would his or her family invest in your venture? Perhaps you are both involved in the start-up anyway.

7. **Friends** – people who believe in you might well be prepared to invest in your business. Several could club together to help you. They might also accept variable repayments linked to how well you're doing.

8. **A man in the pub** – never underestimate those you know, but know little about. The man you drink with might well be a willing investor.

9. **Suppliers** – people who will benefit from your venture may not put in cash but might well lend you equipment or be happy to give you extended credit.

10. **Customers** – your early customers may well be happy to invest in the business and then take their return as discounted product or service. This happens more often than you think!

Dr Hermann Hauser, founder of Acorn Computers and now a venture capitalist in Cambridge, says that the first port of call for anyone looking for additional funding should be 'family and fools'. What he means is that those who have faith in you will be the most likely to invest. Those with money and little common sense should also not be discounted. It is a matter for you and your conscience how far down the 'fools' route you decide to go.

TONY

A graphic designer, Tony needed to invest £5,000 in computer equipment before going solo. Cautious by nature and reluctant to borrow money, he talked with Mark whose printing company his employer worked with from time to time. After swearing him to secrecy, Tony told Mark of his plan and asked for his advice.

What happened was that Mark agreed to buy Tony the computers he needed. In return, Tony would let Mark print the jobs that Tony designed. They agreed to consider the equipment to represent a 2% commission on print, so Tony knew that after introducing £250,000 of print the equipment would be his.

Soon after starting, Tony won a design contract with a large animal charity. Within two years he had fulfilled his obligation and owned his computers. However, he still introduced work to Mark who set aside the 2% commission to fund equipment upgrades for Tony's business.

10 steps to heaven – finding a business angel

Business angels are people who invest in growing enterprises. They've usually made their money from business and so can offer advice as well as cash. Business angels typically lend between £20,000 and £200,000 and are less demanding than venture capital firms who lend more. Business angels know the ropes – here's a checklist to help you tie one down.

1. **Network** – the best angels are often those you meet by being active in local business networks. They tend to keep quiet about the fact that they are investors, so you might know one already and not realise. Let people know you are seeking investment.

2. **Surf** – the internet is a good way to find the national and local business angel networks. These broker introductions between entrepreneurs and angels. Most enable you to register your opportunity and some stage regular 'investment fairs'.

3. **History** – angels like people with track records. Even if you've had the odd disaster or setback, as long as you can demonstrate it was a learning experience then the wisest angels will not be put off. The fact is that you are less likely to fail a second time.

4. **Plan** – your business plan needs to cover all the angles and explain simply and sensibly what you want to achieve. However, angels like simple plans and detailed spreadsheets.

5. **Trading** – angels are really most interested in proven businesses that want to grow. Some will invest in the development of new technology, but only if it's their specialist area.

6. **Profit** – no angel is going to throw money into a deep hole. So if you're up against it and have run out of cash it's unlikely an angel will help.

7. **Opportunity** – have a clear idea why you need money and what it will deliver. Growth for growth's sake is not reason enough, be specific. Have an exit strategy.

8. **Shared risk** – say you've thrown everything you have into the venture and simply need a further £30,000 to reach your corporate climax – your angel will be with you all the way! Once they've invested, an angel usually knows when you need further support.

9. **Compliant** – you need to have all the proper paperwork – copyright and patents, software licences, insurances, etc. Angels do not like nasty surprises.

10. **Passion** – your commitment must be evident and your enthusiasm driven by the opportunity, not the fear of failure. Angels invest in the brave.

If you find networking difficult, or there are few good networking opportunities you can attend, you can often find out about local business angels by:

- asking local accountants, who often have one or two investors as clients;

- talking to business support agencies, who have access to angel networks and can help make introductions;

- finding out who has made a lot of money locally and getting to know them;

- asking suppliers and customers – never rule out investment from them;

- reading press reports about successful people and what interests them

ROBERT

Now in his late fifties, Robert trained as an accountant and successfully led the management buyout of a haulage firm a few years ago. This deal was preceded by a varied and successful career, which made him comfortably off but not rich.

Robert and his wife enjoy life, meeting people and helping in their community. They have no children. Robert enjoys helping young entrepreneurs grow their businesses. At any one time he has money invested in three or four companies. His financial acumen and strategic business eye make him a valuable asset to those he works with. He is a business angel because, he says, it is his way of helping other people achieve the success and satisfaction he has enjoyed himself, as well as giving back something to others. His style is to be firm and friendly. Robert is a typical business angel.

10 ways to do it anyway – without the investment

Everybody expects to need to borrow money to start or grow a business. However, there are alternative, more creative ways to fund your enterprise. Here are ten examples.

1. **Factor debt** – a factor is a company that collects your debts for you and pays you the money as soon as you raise your invoice. They charge a commission and interest, but it gives you positive cash flow. This is important if you are growing quickly.

2. **Take deposits** – many subcontract manufacturing businesses take a 30% deposit before purchasing raw materials. Could you do this too?

3. **Share resources** – don't move to bigger premises straight away, simply find someone with unused space and use that to build capacity. You might also share equipment.

4. **Save other's costs** – sometimes it costs more to mothball plant than it does to operate it. Offer to use and maintain plant for someone no longer needing it.

5. **Buy at auction** – there is always a risk when buying second-hand equipment, but sometimes repossession or bankruptcy sales provide amazing bargains.

6. **Lease** – almost any asset can be leased, which removes the need for upfront investment or bank borrowing. However, make sure you can easily cover the lease payments.

7. **Sell and lease back** – you can sell and lease back existing assets to free up working capital. This can be useful when established businesses want to grow.

8. **Extra shifts** – more and more people are looking for flexible working hours, and not just on the factory floor. Could you get more out of your business if it operated 24 hours a day?

9. **Credit cards** – not often advisable but it can be done. Sign up to lots of new credit cards offering introductory interest-free periods. Be sure to pay them off in good time though!

10. **Take it slowly** – sometimes it is only your impatience that is driving the pace of growth. Growing slowly may take longer but it costs a lot less.

Managing the rate of growth is rather like flying a plane – climb too quickly and you can stall and plunge unexpectedly to earth; climb too gradually and you won't clear the trees at the end of the runway. The business equivalent of stalling a plane is called overtrading. Overtrading is where your sales are growing at an unsustainable pace and customers don't pay you quickly enough to fund your rising costs. Overtrading is one of the major causes of business failure.

You can control the rate of growth of your business by:

- increasing prices as demand grows – to increase profitability and create working capital;

- building a forward order book – of customers prepared to confirm their order and wait;

- focusing your marketing efforts on the most lucrative sectors;

- selling peripheral parts of the business – to raise cash to focus on the core activity;

- referring business that's not for you to other providers in return for a commission.

ROY SUCKLING

A pioneering aviator, Roy started his own airline in 1986 flying one plane between Ipswich and Amsterdam. The business was successful, but the jump to a second plane needed massive investment. Roy discovered that plane builders Dornier had an aircraft repossessed from a failed airline. This was costing money to keep in an airworthy condition. He offered to maintain it for Dornier, fly it and buy it when his cash flow allowed.

To his surprise, Dornier accepted his offer and the business never looked back. Now, more than fifteen years later and after additional investment by a private investor, Roy's company, now called Scot Airways, is one of Britain's most successful small airlines (*www.scotairways.co.uk*).

10 things to avoid at all costs

This book is all about growing your successful business. However, it is a fact that many small businesses go bust and you need to know the warning signs to watch for. Occasionally though, it really is better to throw in the towel and start again.

1. **No cash** – you never seem to have any money in the bank when you need it. Check your costings to see if you are selling too cheap. You may be a 'busy fool'.

2. **Paying late** – stretching payments to suppliers gives only temporary relief to what is usually an underlying lack of profitability. If you must pay late, negotiate the terms.

3. **Falling sales** – if demand falls find out why quickly and either sell more or cut overhead costs. Delaying cost reduction is usually fatal. It's tough, but grasp the nettle!

4. **Tail wagging dog** – you have unwittingly become reliant on one or two large customers and they are starting to screw you down too tightly. You need more customers.

5. **Cash deals** – perhaps you are not drawing a salary and the odd cash deal looks tempting. However, this can damage your reputation and get you into trouble too.

6. **Avoiding the postman** – you'd be surprised how quickly people get used to those nasty letters from angry creditors. Some check the post for cheques and then leave the bills in a pile unopened. Always open the post and face up to what is happening.

7. **Permanent overdraft** – the bank balance, like a cold snap in winter, never rises above zero. Was it always like this? Ask your accountant to look at the figures with you.

8. **The cleaner leaves** – keeping the place tidy has become a luxury you feel you can do without. The workplace becomes depressing and oppressive. It's a downward spiral.

9. **Rumours start** – people talk. If you are struggling it will show and no one wants to trade with a failing company. Quash rumours if you can and try not to behave as if desperate.

10. **The bailiff's calling** – this is the final nail in the coffin lid on your ambition. An aggrieved creditor has the approval of the court to seize your assets. At this point, it's usually game over.

Going bust

OK, so you have a friend whose business is failing (for it cannot happen to you, right?). Here are some pointers that can soften the bump of a business crash.

- **Liability** – if you're a sole trader or partnership, anything you own may be grabbed to settle the business debt. If you're a limited company only the business assets will go, unless you can be proved to have traded wrongfully.

- **Directors** – even if the company has flagrantly traded while insolvent, only directors can be chased for compensation. Remember that this includes all directors, even non-executives. Remember too that action against directors needs to be underwritten by the creditors. If you've no money it's less likely you'll be pursued.

- **Guarantees** – when the end comes, people often find that they've signed all sorts of guarantees along the way. Bank borrowings, company cars, the photocopier and much more may well have been underwritten by you personally. It's not for nothing that a guarantor has often been described as a 'fool with a pen'.

- **Insolvency practitioners** – are accountants who specialise (and are licensed) to unscramble and wind up failed businesses. Most will offer confidential, initial advice free of charge. They will have ideas you don't, so don't delay consulting with one.

- **Voluntary arrangements** – these can avoid total business collapse. Essentially, it's a deal struck between you and your creditors, usually by an insolvency practitioner. Creditors agree to take a percentage of what is owed to them over a period of time, while you trade on and climb out of the mire. Faced with a potential total loss, most creditors welcome voluntary arrangements. They often remain your suppliers.

These are the only two 'negative' pages in this book. Read them, but then focus on the positive aspects of building your business.

6 Branding

choosing business and product names

10 reasons why people will buy from you

People don't buy things for what they are, but for what they will do for them. They need to be convinced that the value of the benefits will outweigh the cost. It doesn't matter what your product or service is, or if you are selling to businesses or consumers. People buy products, not features. Your focus will inevitably be the features as this is where your costs are incurred. When talking to your customers though, always focus on the features. Here are ten good reasons why someone might buy from you.

1. **Meets a need** – the greater the need, the easier the sale. For example, you'll be keen to find a glazier if you have a broken window.

2. **Highly desirable** – you don't need it all the time, but right now it's really appealing and readily available. This is why ice cream sells well on the beach in summer.

3. **Affordable** – your customer has the money, or you have broken the cost down into manageable instalments.

4. **Safe** – your product is reliable and perhaps reduces a risk that worries the customer.

5. **Performance** – it does what it says on the box. Reputation and evidence of performance, perhaps testimonials, will reassure your customers and have them saying yes.

6. **Appearance** – it looks good. Given the choice, no one would buy an ugly product if one that looked more appealing was available. Also, does it make the customer look good?

7. **Convenience** – is it easy to use, easy to find and easy to dispose of afterwards?

8. **Economy** – once you've bought it how cheap will it be to run? A more concentrated product might cost more but be cheaper to use as you need less of it each time.

9. **Durability** – the lifespan of a product often dictates its value for money. The cheapest often does not last as long as the most expensive. Spell it out to your customers.

10. **Peer pressure** – nobody likes to feel left behind. This applies to business purchases such as PDAs, where people buy them to be fashionable and not because they need one.

Understanding the difference between features and benefits is a key point. Too many people promote features and forget the benefits. Imagine you are buying a van. Here are some possible features and benefits.

Feature	Benefit
Carries two tonnes	More deliveries possible per day
Diesel engine	Lower fuel cost per mile, more economical
Weighs less than 7.5 tonnes	You don't need a truck driving licence
White paintwork	Easy to fix promotional vinyls

You must always listen to what your customers are saying about your product or service. Sometimes, what they say will surprise or even offend you. However, if your motive for being in business is to make money (and it should be) you need to listen and adapt to meet their changing demands. You have to give people what they want, as well as what they need.

WILLIAM WRIGLEY

In the 1880s William Wrigley started a business selling laundry soap. He was very proud of his soap and to encourage people to buy it he gave away free chewing gum with every bar. The trouble was that, while people loved the gum, they were not particularly impressed with the soap. William then had three choices:

- improve the soap and stop messing about with promotional gifts;
- ditch the soap and sell chewing gum instead;
- soldier on regardless, for surely others would soon come to value his soap.

Of course, William took the second option and chewing gum can now be found stuck to pavements and bus seats the world over. He changed direction completely and made his fortune. He listened to his customers.

10 tips when choosing a name

It's sometimes easier to choose a name for a baby than for a business, product or service. Naming a baby is very personal, but the names you choose at work have to appeal to other people and customers, rather than to yourself. Here are ten tips to help you choose names.

1. **Be specific** – there really is nothing better than making it obvious what you do and why you're better. Economy Car Hire, for example, or Rapid Radiator Repairs.

2. **Positive associations** – link the name to something well known in common usage (so not copyright), for example Capability Brown's Garden Store.

3. **Top of the list** – while Aardvark Roofing might get you pole position in Yellow Pages, it'll be suspiciously obvious that you've done it on purpose. Better to create a happy coincidence, such as Abbey Roofing.

4. **Generics** – you would remember a business called Wellington's Boot Store. Also, if people are searching for you online, generic names help.

5. **Humour** – used carefully humour can make a name more memorable. Belt and Braces Access Platform Hire suggests that safety is a key feature of the customer offer.

6. **Homophones** – these are words that sound the same but have different spellings. They stick in the mind, for example The Sauce Source Ltd.

7. **Numbers** – using numbers passes in and out of fashion. Unless there is a good reason (M25 Auto Recovery) numbers are usually best avoided.

8. **Your name(s)** – although Messrs Marks, Spencer, Ford and Woolworth are among the best known exceptions, it usually shows a lack of imagination to simply call your business by your name. This is especially important if your name is difficult to say.

9. **Domain name** – the internet is becoming more important. Check out the available domain names before committing yourself.

10. **Get a second opinion** – hours of hard work will lead you to some stunning ideas for names. But before deciding, ask others for their view.

Of course, it's not always possible to have the name you want and first thought of. This is often because you will previously have heard names and phrases that are not available but are safely stowed in your subconscious mind. Most major brand names are protected by copyright, as are similar names. To avoid the risk of litigation it's usually best to steer clear of well-known names. You can check registered patents free online.

Conversely, you also want to stake a claim to your business or product name because others might try to copy you when you are successful. This whole area is called 'intellectual property' and is a potential legal minefield unless you are guided by an expert. Here are the basics.

- Trade marks™ – anyone can put the ™ symbol next to their product name or logo. All it means is that the owner considers it to be a trade mark and wishes to make people aware of the fact. It costs nothing to do but affords limited protection from plagiarists.

- Registered marks ® – trade mark agents can help you register your brand names and logos. You can threaten to sue anyone who tries to copy you. The ® says this.

- Copyright © – the mark means that the piece of work thus marked is the property of the author and cannot be reproduced without permission. Again it costs nothing to do.

- Patent – patent agents can work with you to protect that part of your product or process that is unique and specific to you. The registration process is lengthy and can be expensive. However, if you are developing something new that has great potential, you should patent it. Business angels and other investors will expect you to own patents.

SUPERMACS

Teacher Pat McDonagh saw an opportunity to create a fast-food chain in Ireland. He chose the nickname he was given at school, Supermac – a tribute to Malcolm MacDonald, then a popular footballer with Newcastle United. His first outlet opened in County Galway offering typically Irish meals to his customers, as well as wider international fare.

The business now has more than 50 outlets throughout Ireland with sales exceeding €70m a year. With a population of only 3 million people, you can see that Supermacs has cornered the market. The company name is coincidentally similar to a well-known US fast-food chain. Not surprisingly, Supermacs is a registered trade mark.

10 ways to test your new idea

However much your enthusiasm is encouraging you to rush ahead, it's always worthwhile taking the time to test your new idea before committing yourself fully. Here are ten simple ways to test your new idea before you've spent too much.

1. **Ask a friend** – this is yet another time when the honest view of a trusted friend can save you lots of wasted effort and money. Tell them to be blunt, honest and explain why.

2. **Ask a customer** – showing potential buyers mock-ups, prototypes, etc. is a great way to involve them in your development work. Show them alternatives and have them say why they prefer one over the other. Hopefully this will also get you some early orders.

3. **Blog** – find and join a suitable internet forum and blog your idea. Invite feedback.

4. **Seek editorial** – your new idea might be newsworthy. Asking editors of the trade journals your customers read to profile you and your concept will stimulate comment, and perhaps enquiries too. The editor's feedback is as valuable as that of readers.

5. **Ask ad agencies** – advertising agency folk spend their whole lives thinking of ways to market new things. Invite three agencies to pitch for your project. Their questions, comments and ideas will shape your thinking. If one of them has some brilliant ideas, hire them.

6. **Street surveys** – stopping people in the street and soliciting their views is a great way to test a consumer business idea. Seek permission before doing this in a private shopping mall. In general, people are happy to pause and share their opinions.

7. **Focus groups** – facilitated focus groups can get people thinking about and discussing your idea. The group literally thinks of the answers you want. Some researchers have special rooms where the meeting can be recorded for transcription and later analysis.

8. **Look elsewhere** – there's not much that's new and your idea is probably being exploited elsewhere. Use the internet to find similar enterprises that you can examine.

9. **Read research** – academics somewhere are probably researching in your business area. Delve into academic internet forums and read what's being said.

10. Just do it – sometimes your instinct will be right whatever your market testing tells you. If you decide to 'just do it' make sure you limit your risk.

Large organisations spend large amounts of money researching new ideas and opportunities. They don't always get it right. The motor industry is a good example. Quite a few new car models are developed, manufactured and launched only to be cut from the range within a year or two. This is a costly way to test the market and one that the small business can rarely afford to adopt. Here are some questions to ask yourself when developing your new idea.

- How much will it cost to develop?
- How big is the potential market?
- What external trends make me think that now is the right time?
- How will I fund it?
- What will it replace?
- How many do I need to make/provide to break even?
- Will people repeat purchase?
- Who might buy this business from me when it's established?
- What am I really trying to prove here?
- Could I do it more simply?

BEN

Having worked for two design companies since graduating, Ben found he didn't like the way people in his sector tended to use jargon to confuse the client and inflate the invoice. He recognised that integrity and trust were just as important as creativity in building long-term client relationships.

He decided to start his own agency with graphic designer and good friend Dave. They called their business 'Naked Marketing' because nothing was hidden from the client. Within a year, it was clear that people respected their openness and willingness to tell it like it was. They have many clients in the public and voluntary sectors and face a great future.

Their new idea was simply to communicate in words that their clients, usually non-marketers, would understand. It was simple, they tested it with people they knew and then followed their instinct. They now have a very successful, growing business.

10 design tips to bring your idea to life

Many of us 'think' in pictures and everyone is strongly influenced by images – that's why advertising images can be so powerful. Your business, your product and the benefits you deliver will carry more weight if they are illustrated visually. You might choose to commission a graphic designer to help. Here are ten design tips to help you.

1. **Pictures save words** – people like to see pictures of products. Even better is seeing people like them who are clearly benefiting from the experience.

2. **Endorsements add weight** – if you commission photography for your promotional material, why not try to feature a famous person. Their endorsement will add weight.

3. **Sense of place** – the setting for photography is vital. Choose unusual locations that will appeal to your target audience and emphasise the benefits you are offering.

4. **Faces and hands** – make images human by showing faces and hands. Use happy people!

5. **Words** – make sure you use a legible typeface and that the print is large enough to see. Avoid using capital letters as these are harder to read.

6. **Colour counts** – green suggests environment, red aggression and blue cold. Look at ads for organic products, sports cars and refrigeration and you'll see examples. Choose colours that suit the messages you're trying to convey.

7. **Consistency** – once you've got a logo or style, use it everywhere – letterheads, website, clothing and vehicles. It may seem contrived to you but it will reassure your customers.

8. **Serifs** – these are the little tails that appear on characters in some typefaces. The experts say that serifs make text easier to read as they carry the eye from letter to letter.

9. **Brevity** – promotional material should contain short passages of text made up of short sentences using simple words. Remember you are fighting to hold attention.

10. **Be explicit** – do not beat about the bush; state the benefit argument clearly and simply.

The design brief

When seeking the help of a graphic designer, it helps to have a really clear idea of what you want done. Here are some questions you might be asked.

- What is the product or service you are offering and how does it work?
- How is it different from its competitors?
- Who buys it now?
- Who do you want to reach and why?
- What do you want your potential customers to KNOW about:
  - your business?
  - your products or services?
  - your offer? (It can be good to create 'special offers' to raise interest.)
- What do you want your potential customers to THINK about:
  - benefits they'll gain?
  - value for money?
  - urgency – why is it important to buy now?
- What do you want your potential customers to DO:
  - visit a website?
  - give you a ring?
  - visit your outlet?
  - fill in and post a coupon?
- How much do you want to spend?
- What would you consider to be a good response?

Your website

Remember that your prospective customers will expect to learn more from your website that they can from advertising or brochures. Your website needs to match other materials and also:

- give more technical, detailed information for those who want it;
- capture each visitor's contact details before allowing them to download detailed data. This means that you can follow them up by e-mail.

7 Sales

how to help more people say yes!

10 ways that people could buy from you

The easier you make it for people to find you and do business with you, the more business you will do. Marketing is only one aspect of that challenge. Here are ten opportunities you might create for your potential customers.

1. **Retail** – some people will prefer to buy direct. This is true even if you also supply a wide range of outlets. It's why many who make consumer goods also have a 'factory shop'.

2. **Wholesale** – when you sell into the trade, the trade become your customer and the user of your product the consumer. You can sell a higher volume, albeit at a lower margin. Economies of scale, however, may mean your cost per unit is lower so you're better off overall.

3. **Mail order** – you post information to people who might be interested and they either accept your offer or throw your mailing in the bin. Make sure your list contains people with a high probability of being interested in your offer.

4. **From an agent** – agents sell products and services from a range of suppliers. You pay commission but, unlike a sales team, agents cost you only when successful.

5. **Online** – anyone in the world can buy from you if you have a website. People can pay online using their credit card and then download or be mailed your product or service.

6. **By recommendation** – a satisfied customer recommends you to their friends.

7. **Networking** – some people sell only through networking. As well as attending business breakfasts and other organised networking events, good networkers pop up everywhere!

8. **At an event** – if there's a conference or fair that you think will attract your target audience, why not take a stand and let people meet you or see what you produce?

9. **Multilevel** – multilevel marketing is where each customer is encouraged to become a distributor, recruiting you more customers. It is tightly regulated but very effective.

10. **As a package** – sometimes others have products or services that complement your own. Collaborating to develop a package can generate interest and business for you both.

Of course, the opportunities you offer to your prospective customers will largely depend on the business you are in. For example:

- Selling direct is best when:
  - you only need a few large orders;
  - your product or service is complex or bespoke;
  - you are trading locally where reputation is everything;
  - there are few alternatives so people have to come to you.

- Selling via others is best when:
  - you want to roll out your product quickly;
  - established distributor/retail networks already have the customers;
  - you prefer not to recruit a large number of salespeople;
    your product adds more value when sold with something else.

- Selling online is best when:
  - your market is small, specialist and widely spread;
  - you are confident you can attract visitors to your website;
  - you want to sell to members of online networks and communities;
  - your product has a low unit cost and is easy to deliver.

ALISTAIR built a business publishing guides to 'upmarket' B&B accommodation. The guides are produced annually and are distributed via the book trade. Accommodation owners pay to be listed in his guides, although he only lists them after one of his inspectors has visited and is satisfied they meet the high standard his readers have come to expect.

The internet has revolutionised his business. You can now search his website for accommodation as well as purchase copies of his printed guides. While this has reduced sales through the book trade, this is more than compensated for by his ability to list new accommodation as soon as it has been inspected. By giving his customers a choice between printed guides and an interactive website he has grown his audience. His website also contains a blog where he shares his thoughts. This makes the relationship with each customer feel more personal. Customers feel more involved than they did before.

10 ways to close more sales

Selling is the energy that fuels your business. Every business needs new customers as, over time, customers leave. Being able to sell means that you can control the flow of new business and confidently fund your future. Here are ten simple ways to become better at closing sales.

1. **Buy** – reflect on what it is that makes *you* buy. What do you like salespeople to say to you? Do they show genuine interest? Learn by buying. (But don't spend too much!)

2. **Read** – there are many good books on sales techniques. Read one, but do not inhibit your natural style or personality. Remember you need to appear confident and relaxed.

3. **Listen** – people will only give you the time of day if they have decided that what you are offering is interesting. Ask them what they want from you. Let them do the hard work!

4. **Know** – your rivals' products or services inside out. Never knock them, simply focus on the differences that support your case. Remember that no two customers are the same.

5. **Persist** – some people take a while to make a decision. Keep in touch, don't give up.

6. **Care** – think of your prospects as human beings and not orders waiting to be placed. Show that your interest in them is genuine and from the heart.

7. **Reassure** – build confidence in you and what you are selling. Be helpful, not pushy.

8. **Illustrate** – pictures can say more than words. Invest in good 'action' photography.

9. **Visit** – encourage your prospects to meet existing customers. Make the introduction and then let them talk about you when you're not there.

10. **Believe** – if you are passionate that you are offering the best option to your customers, you will succeed. If you're only after the cash it'll be much harder. You must believe.

You don't necessarily have to be well versed in the stages of the sale to succeed at selling. Sometimes the so-called professional salesperson comes over as being just a little too glib to be totally believable. In fact, some of the most successful salespeople don't conform at all. Instead they win business through determination, character and, sometimes, even cheek!

A good way to think about how you are going to sell is to consider the reasons why people buy. A good mnemonic to help you remember is the word SPACED. Each letter represents a common reason for buying – what salespeople call a buying motive:

Security – is this safe and will it work?

Performance – will it meet my needs?

Appearance – does it look good? Will buying it make me look good?

Convenience – is it easy to introduce and use, or will it cause me problems?

Economical – can I afford to run it? How much will it save me?

Durability – will it last long enough for me to recoup the investment?

JAMIE is sales director for a firm that supplies photocopiers and office supplies. His marketplace has changed dramatically over the past few years. To really benefit from the machines he sells, his customers need to learn to use their copier as a network printer. However, human nature being what it is, people are reluctant to let go of their trusty old laser printers to embrace the latest technology.

To make it easy for people to see the cost saving, Jamie provides a spreadsheet that allows them to work out what they are currently paying for printing and compare this cost with that of the new technology. The figures they calculate usually makes Jamie's solution look good value.

Jamie works hard to sell the value of working out the cost of printing. His customers then sell themselves the idea that a new copier will save them money.

10 ways that distributors can add value

It is often tempting to try to sell direct and avoid sharing your profits with a distributor – in some sectors they demand a 50% margin. However, distributors often have an existing relationship with your potential audience and can sell far higher volumes of your product or service than you can on your own. Here are ten valuable benefits that distributors can offer.

1. **Customers** – they are already supplying people with the potential to buy your product, otherwise why would they stock it? Commit them to a sales target.

2. **Knowledge** – builders, farmers and other merchants stock everyone's products. While unlikely to betray confidences, distributors can give you valuable product and pricing advice because they also sell for rivals. They will tell you if you're too expensive.

3. **Shop window** – many distributors operate retail outlets. They can literally provide a shop window to display your products.

4. **Credit control** – by selling to distributors you reduce your risk of bad debt. The distributor has to collect payment from all their customers. You bill the distributor.

5. **Stockholding** – many will have warehousing and be prepared to take your product as you make it, reducing your need to store finished goods.

6. **Delivery** – by delivering your products at the same time as they deliver others, transport costs are lower than if you delivered direct yourself.

7. **Language** – if you want to sell overseas, working with a local distributor who understands the language and business culture is usually the only way.

8. **Credibility** – if you provide professional services distributors and intermediaries can win you work by staking their reputation on your ability.

9. **Two bites** – you can have two bites from one market if you sell your distributors an 'own brand' version of your branded product. By offering choice you sell more.

10. **Feedback** – when testing new ideas your distributor's sales team can assess the market by simply discussing the idea with their customers.

Distributors, however, are not a panacea for all marketing challenges. In some sectors your distributors will want you to invest significantly in their marketing activity. Alternatively they might only work for you if you can encourage new customers to come to them, which means consumer marketing. The key is to negotiate a 'business plan' with each distributor.

Managing distributors

There is an art to managing distributors effectively. They must be motivated, informed and supported. Equally they should not become so vital to your existence that they can call the shots. Here are five ingredients from which you and your distributors can create a recipe for success.

- **Agree targets** – the more considered and detailed the targets, the more you will both focus on achieving them. Product mix, pricing, sales per month and level of support can all be targeted and measured.

- **Product knowledge** – people only sell what they feel they understand. Provide literature and sales aids to help them to explain the benefits.

- **Incentives** – underpin key targets with incentives. These can be additional margins for the company or target-related rewards for their salespeople.

- **Review** – both sides should review progress against the targets regularly and discuss how to make up any shortfalls.

- **Campaigns** – short, sharp campaigns focusing on a single product or opportunity can get you a greater share of the distributor's attention for a short spell.

10 good things about selling direct

Sometimes it makes sense to sell direct to the user of your product or service. Here are ten benefits of selling direct.

1. **Few customers** – if you need only a small number of customers, as is often the case in a business-to-business environment, distributors won't sell enough to add value.

2. **Relationships** – if you are providing a personal service, for example as a life coach, people are buying *you*. You are the service and will win new customers because of it.

3. **Referral generators** – some businesses, for example home improvements, win almost all their new business from people introduced by satisfied customers. Encourage this.

4. **You're in touch** – if you or your staff talk to customers you get to hear pretty quickly if things in your marketplace change.

5. **Control** – if you're someone who feels that no one else can do the job as well as you then selling direct is your opportunity to prove this to yourself. Remember, it's your business and you must be happy with it.

6. **Specialist** – perhaps people will only buy from you because you have expert knowledge. If this is the case get others to do everything else so you can just talk to customers.

7. **Loyalty** – if you hire and develop your own sales team they will spend all of their time selling for you. No distributor can give you that level of commitment.

8. **Negotiate down** – you can be more flexible when selling direct. Distributors, quite rightly, need to refer back to you before deviating too far from your agreed trading terms. Sometimes it's right to 'have a deal' and get the order.

9. **Negotiate up** – everyone encounters opportunities to take an order at a higher margin. When your distributor does this he is unlikely to share the extra profit with you.

10. **Sell extras** – in some markets, once the order has been taken, you can add profitable extras to the deal. Remember, the most important thing about any sale is the total profit it generates for your business.

Recognising that your enthusiasm coupled with your belief in your product or service are the most important factors, it's useful to have a track to follow when you're making your sales presentation. Here are the stages most sales interviews go through:

- **Approach** – you need to get in front of your prospect. This means identifying people likely to be interested in what you have to offer and getting yourself in front of them.

- **Rapport** – tuning in to the same wavelength is vital. Good salespeople do this through their introduction and through showing an interest in the customer and their needs.

- **Probe** – by asking open questions (those that cannot be answered yes or no) you find out which issues you might be able to solve. By probing you can identify specific opportunities for your product or service. Your questioning directs the conversation.

- **Proposition** – having established what the need is, you now explain (or better still, show) how your solution is the best. Use benefits (what it does) not features (what it is) to paint a positive picture in the mind of your potential customer. Value must outweigh the cost.

- **Close** – having discussed how your answer is perhaps the right one, you go for commitment – quite simply, you ask for the order. Use closed questions (that can only be answered yes or no) to seek commitment.

- **Follow-up** – once you've got the order be sure to do what you have promised to the customer. Otherwise all the hard work will have been wasted.

The same process is used when phoning to arrange sales appointments. The difference is that you are selling the idea of a meeting, not your product or service.

Top sales tip

Offering two alternatives makes saying 'no' more difficult – for example, 'Would you like us to deliver on Wednesday or Thursday?' 'Would you prefer it in blue or green?'

10 ways to sell even more

Selling is not a mechanical process, it is more a focused conversation where all participants have agreed the topic. As well as following a logical sequence, you need to respond to your prospect in recognising opportunities to get closer to agreement. Here are ten more sales tips.

1. **Ask why** – if your prospect turns you down. Not only do you need to know the reason, but you also want an opportunity to overcome their objection.

2. **Ask who** – the moment you have the order is the best time to ask for a recommendation or referral. Too many people wait – do it straight away.

3. **Drop cards** – business cards are cheap advertising. Always carry cards and never hold back from presenting one.

4. **Get about** – develop a profile in your industry or sector. Attend the events that your customers attend. Ask good questions of speakers you hear. Be noticed.

5. **Be memorable** – some of the best business people have a physical 'trade mark'. Branson doesn't wear a tie, others always wear a bow tie. Stand out from the crowd.

6. **Read everything** – once you develop the habit of reading press articles, office noticeboards, even invoices on your customers' desks, you will become more aware of what you can do to increase your sales. Learn to translate what you read into opportunity.

7. **Never stop** – customers have a home life too. When you bump into people you do business with in the supermarket make a point of speaking to them, but not about work!

8. **Say your name** – whenever you meet someone say your name as you introduce yourself. This both spares embarrassment and makes it easier for people to remember you.

9. **Signs** – signwritten vans and other 'point of delivery' advertising are good ways of getting noticed, particularly if you sell to householders. Be easy to identify.

10. **Make news** – get to know the journalists who write for your marketplace. Keep them fed with stories about your business. Be helpful and responsive, and enjoy more publicity.

Networks

Too often, people say they've not got the time to network. In most businesses, networking is vitally important. Success is often really all about 'who you know'. Here are some types of network and good reasons for joining them.

- Chambers of Commerce include membership organisations covering a local area:
  - keep you informed of local issues and opportunities;
  - have members who may be potential customers;
  - have active members always in the news – so become active!

- Breakfast networking clubs usually meet weekly. They:
  - follow an established format where everyone gets to speak,
  - positively encourage members to provide leads for each other;
  - offer training sessions to build confidence and presentation skills.

- Trade associations lobby on behalf of and support business sectors. They have:
  - active members who hear about new initiatives first;
  - members who can build their profile through sponsorship or committee work;
  - access to research and industry data that can keep your business on track.

- Professional institutes are useful because:
  - their active members tend to be the most progressive/ambitious;
  - being an event speaker enables you to demonstrate your understanding;
  - if your competitors are also members you have an opportunity to talk.

HIMU is a consultant who helps organisations to develop robust quality systems. He chairs a local business group that meets monthly. The group has around 50 members from a wide range of business backgrounds.

Because Himu puts a lot of energy into making the business group a success, everyone respects him. They also know what he does for a living and much of his work results from informal introductions made by network members.

Himu knows that his time spent running the business group is time well spent.

10 ways to network

For many people, networking is a daunting prospect. It means approaching and talking with complete strangers. Here are ten tips to help you get started.

1. **Know what you want** – you need to network with people who you can benefit from knowing. Only go to networking events that you feel will be relevant to your situation.

2. **Elevator pitch** – this is simply your prepared introduction. Be comfortable explaining who you are, what you do, why you're different and what you're seeking – in two minutes.

3. **Volunteer** – whatever you join, become active. Become a committee member, create opportunities for people to need to talk to you. Invest time and energy.

4. **Ask questions** – everybody likes to talk about themselves. Get people talking and then steer the conversation towards your areas of interest. Don't look bored.

5. **Look the part** – what you wear says a lot about you. Try not to dress like everybody else. Invest in the services of a good image consultant – the results can be amazing!

6. **Be memorable** – carry business cards and offer them freely. You want people to remember you when they get back to work. Also make sure you wear a name badge.

7. **Shake hands** – always greet people with a smile and a firm, but not too tight, handshake. Look them in the eye as you say 'hello' – you'll appear more confident.

8. **Eat first** – it's difficult to talk with your mouth full. Eat before you go and politely nibble rather than load your plate. You're there to network, not fill your belly.

9. **Move on** – don't spend the entire event with one person. To move on without seeming rude, touch their arm as you make your excuse to leave. Avoid looking over their shoulder and drifting off when you spot someone else you'd rather talk to.

10. **Take notes** – take a moment to record what you've said, heard or promised to do – otherwise you'll have forgotten by tomorrow morning.

Networking is rather like a bank savings account – you have to make several deposits before you can hope to earn interest and make a withdrawal. There are several business networking clubs you might consider joining. Some are specific to an area or industry, others form part of national and international networks. For example, if you joined the local branch of one of the large breakfast networking organisations you would probably find:

- up to 50 people who meet on the same morning every week;
- no direct competitors, as most limit membership to one per business sector;
- an opportunity to talk every week about what you're looking for;
- regular opportunities to talk to the group about what you do;
- networking training sessions;
- members committed to introducing each other to new customers.

Online networks provide an almost overwhelming array of people you can network with. Most have a search facility to enable you to identify common interests, and various forums where you can debate pertinent issues.

In some cities you will also find professional networking facilitators. These are individuals or firms who arrange events at which people can meet each other. These are rather like dating agencies in the way that they work, except business is the objective rather than pleasure.

CHRIS

A skilled computer network engineer, meeting new people is not one of Chris's favourite activities. He's rather shy and prefers to get on with the job than engage in small talk. A friend introduced him to a breakfast networking group.

Chris found that because there was structure to the meetings, where everyone had their two minutes to speak, he felt more comfortable. Over time many of the members of the group became good friends. This made it an even more relaxed networking environment.

Members of Chris's breakfast networking group regularly introduce him to new customers and he does the same for them. He enjoys networking in this setting.

8 Profits

estimating and recording costs, especially your time

10 ways to find more time

It's all too easy to fill your diary with things to do, but are they taking the place of more important tasks you're simply putting off? Here are ten ways to get more done each day.

1. **Make a list** – at the end of each day, list in order of priority things you must do tomorrow. Listing it now gets your morning off to a flying start.

2. **Have treats** – we're all human so working flat out 24/7 will not produce the best results. Save some nice tasks you really enjoy as treats to celebrate finishing the chores.

3. **Be realistic** – do not budget to fill every working hour. At least 20% of your time will be taken up with admin, queries and problem-solving.

4. **Make Friday special** – do not let work spill over into the weekend. Use Friday afternoon to tie up the week's loose ends. You need the weekend to relax.

5. **Do what you love** – if you love your work, it won't feel like work. If you hate your work then why did you start this business? Have you lost sight of your original vision?

6. **Time to think** – the old cliché about working in your business rather than on it rings true for most of us. Walk on the beach, sit in the park. Reflect, consider, stop and think!

7. **Avoid distraction** – switch off Outlook, put voicemail on and focus on one key task. Those interruptions are costing you time. Deal with them all together when you're ready.

8. **Clear the desk** – do not pile up your tasks on the desk or workshop bench. Put things away (or throw them out) and have only your current work in front of you.

9. **Buy a stop watch** – time your phone calls. Chatting builds relationships but are you really wasting time? Timing your calls will tend to make them shorter.

10. **Fill the bin** – every business receives tonnes of mail and most of it is junk. Sort it as it arrives. Act on what's important and recycle the junk mail. Don't hoard paper.

Sometimes, however well you manage your time others will waste it for you. Few of the time-management books out there seem to recognise this, yet it can be a real problem. For example, if you own a corner shop you might be the only person a lonely customer talks to all day – they've all the time in the world. Equally challenging are those people we meet from large organisations – perhaps they are your suppliers. These people can be preoccupied with office or industry politics and will delight in sharing their theories with you. You need to discourage this, without seeming rude. Here are five ways to stop other people wasting your time.

- **Agree an agenda** – if it's an arranged meeting, e-mail over your objectives and any background info first to help the other person prepare. Let them add to the agenda too.

- **45 minutes** – most business meetings last an hour. The most successful people, however, start their meetings by stating that they have only 45 minutes. Try it – you'll find you all get to the point quicker.

- **Be assertive** – use selling skills to control the conversation and gain commitment at each stage of the meeting. Avoid beating around the bush and say it like it is.

- **Summarise** – frequent summarising by the meeting leader cuts out excess debate. Sometimes everyone is actually in agreement, but do not recognise the fact. Summarise and seek consensus, then move on.

- **Steal minutes** – sometimes meetings go really well and you get the business done really quickly. Don't then fill the spare time with needless conversation, end the meeting early.

10 ways to work out your true costs

Understanding your costs will enable you to set your prices accurately. Many businesses, particularly very new ones, get this wrong and do not cover all of their costs with their sales. Understanding your costs is as important as understanding your customers. Here are ten tips.

1. **Timesheets** – keeping timesheets may seem like a chore but it soon becomes a habit. Know how much time you spend on a job and be able to prove it to your customer.

2. **Budget** – create a detailed cash-flow budget for your business. See the impact on your profitability if sales fall short but costs remain high.

3. **Overheads** – these are costs you're committed to even if you sell nothing. They need to be built in to your sales price. Most people do this as a percentage.

4. **Mark-up** – many businesses like to roll all their costs into a mark-up on their time; car repair workshops are a good example. Check your next bill and see for yourself.

5. **Finance** – it's easy to overlook bank and interest charges, plus loan arrangement fees, in your overhead costs. Don't forget them – they will need to be paid.

6. **Bad debts** – if you suffer from bad debts, build a figure into your pricing so that all customers are covering the occasional non-payer. Budget for bad debts.

7. **Good buying** – make one person responsible for buying. It keeps it simple and stops everyone ordering stuff you can't track. You don't want to carry too much stock.

8. **Purchase orders** – having a piece of paper your bookkeeper can match with a supplier's invoice prevents accidental overpayments if supplier invoices are wrong.

9. **Add what's new** – constantly review your costs. If things go up in price then reflect this in the prices you charge.

10. **Benchmark** – find others in your business sector and share data. Find out where their costs are lower. Trade organisations often do this for their members.

As a business grows, it moves from being informal to organised – or at least it should! In the early days, the founder usually keeps everything in their head. As activity grows this becomes harder and systems are needed. Setting up systems can be quite a headache for it means analysing what has been going on in the business so far. This process can reveal a few surprises!

Without going over the top, it makes sound sense to put simple systems in place at the beginning. Initially this will only back up what you already know, but as your business starts to grow you'll find that these systems become more important.

Key points to remember are that:

- purchase orders are as important as invoices if you are to avoid mistakes;
- a simple spreadsheet that you update monthly is a good starting point.
- SAGE™ accounts software provides valuable management reports.

JACKIE was a social worker. She became interested in aromatherapy massage and the way that this technique calmed severely disturbed people. Unfortunately, her employer could not fund her to do this work all the time so she decided to go freelance.

She had a network of potential customers. Most were care homes that look after people with behavioural problems. Many were also secure units where residents are not allowed out.

To calculate her selling price she simply divided her previous salary by the number of people she could work with. She was soon very busy, but never seemed to have any money.

Then a friend pointed out that the care homes benefited enormously from the work she did. Residents were calmer and easier to manage. She increased her price and nobody complained. Now she is building a team so that more people can be helped.

10 expensive surprises you face as you grow

When you are growing a business it's a battle to keep costs under control as your sales grow. The euphoria of sales success can lull you into a sense of false security making investment seem sensible. Here are ten surprises to avoid.

1. **Overpromising** – we all do it. A customer places a huge order and wants delivery really quickly. To keep them happy you agree – then lose money doing the impossible.

2. **Underdelivering** – you're busy and you cut corners. Work quality slips, mistakes slip through unnoticed and soon customers, and your reputation, begin to slip away.

3. **Paperwork gets left** – in the rush to complete the job you cut a few corners and, surprise surprise, the work is not quite up to scratch.

4. **Slow suppliers** – you become so busy working that you don't get round to raising invoices. Cash flow suffers as a consequence.

5. **Late payers** – the customer of your dreams becomes a haunting nightmare. Let down and disappointed, they stall on payment while arguing on quality.

6. **Learning curve** – you hire more staff to meet the demand but they take ages to train and output falls as your existing people help them learn. Your costs rise but not your output.

7. **Space race** – with all the extra staff, stock and equipment suddenly there's no room. Temperatures rise, the car park is full and everybody starts to moan.

8. **Systems squeak** – perhaps you've used a manual job card system or rudimentary accounts software. All this extra work means you need to upgrade. That takes time!

9. **Time travels** – the hands on the clock spin round and you seem to be on an accelerating treadmill. As you get busier, things can actually take you longer. You're very tired.

10. **Partner's panic** – all of a sudden, just when everything that can go wrong seems to, you get home and are met with a barrage of anxious questions from the love of your life.

Of course, growing a business is not all bad news. You simply have to be alert to the fact that unless you've invested in people, plant and processes before winning those extra sales then it's going to be tough for a while. Few successful entrepreneurs built their businesses that way. Most accepted the orders first and then invested in the capacity to meet them.

Here are some of the positive things you can do to limit the downside of growth.

- **Schedule** – scheduling your work using specialist software, a spreadsheet or even a calendar on the wall enables you to allocate time and resources and to plan when things are needed. Tell customers when their job is scheduled so they know when you expect to deliver. Try building a forward order book – you may not need to do everything at once.

- **Communicate** – think about how leading e-commerce sites like Amazon e-mail to confirm your order and expected delivery, and then again when the order is dispatched. If there's a problem you are informed straight away. You cannot be angry because you are kept informed – the firm is honest and realistic. How could you communicate better?

- **Evaluate** – take time to look back on each job you do. Did you complete it within the budgeted material cost and time? (Did you measure the time it took?) Only by looking at what has happened can you change what will happen in the future. Create a culture of continuous improvement.

HELEN manages and runs a business concerned with luxury ski chalets in the French Alps. Her customers tend to be successful people and can, she says, be very discerning. Very much a perfectionist, Helen enjoyed predicting and planning for every possible eventuality.

However, this made it difficult to grow the business as she was always so busy. She made time to network with other business people so that she could understand how they managed to grow their businesses. Helen found that, while it was nice to give a Rolls-Royce service, most customers were just as happy with less.

By focusing on the aspects of service that her customers value most, she has found time to do more. Helen's business has started to grow.

10 profitable extras to put on the bill

With so many of the things we buy it is the extras that make the profit for the provider. What's more, it is often the optional extras that differentiate the product in the marketplace. Cars and first-class travel are good examples. Here are ten extras almost any business can offer.

1. **Morning delivery** – people will pay extra for quicker delivery. All you do is rearrange your driver's route to go there first. Your costs stay the same but the profits rise.

2. **Changes** – every time a customer has a change of mind it creates work. Even if it doesn't, make it obvious that it's a change and charge for it. People will pay for changes.

3. **Overtime** – if you have to incur higher labour costs to meet customers' deadlines, should they not pay more? You can often charge more for a 'rushed job'.

4. **Assembly** – so many people just do what they always do and forget to look for opportunities. If you make components why not see if you can handle assembly as well.

5. **Disbursements** – solicitors have a wonderful way of recording every phone call and postage stamp – and then calling them 'disbursements' and charging. Do the same.

6. **Packaging** – environmental legislation makes packaging disposal a real headache for many. If you make regular deliveries, collect used packaging and recycle or reuse.

7. **Just ask** – Indian restaurants seem to offer you extras instinctively – poppadoms, pickles, side dishes, more beer. They understand that the more they offer, the more you will buy.

8. **Assume** – add things to the order and give the customer the chance to opt out – most will buy. A good example is the travel insurance added by online rail ticket sellers.

9. **Time** – this is your biggest cost. If a job is completed in less time than you estimated do not automatically pass the saving on to the customer. Benefit from your efficiency.

10. **Offer choices** – even if two options cost you the same, you can always ask more for the most popular. Price should be linked to demand, not costs.

The golden rule when pricing your work is to always base your price on market conditions. Too many people simply tally up their costs and add a margin. You will find that if you set your prices to reflect market conditions, some things you make or sell will earn you more than others. That's fine and, at times, you can use part of this extra margin to encourage people to try new products. This is achieved by offering 'buy one get one free' or similar deals.

You therefore need a range of products or services to be able to give your customers choice. By giving choices, you make it harder for them to say no. Your product or service ranges should contain:

- a low cost, entry level option – allowing new customers a low risk trial;
- a high cost, top flight option – making everything else look better value;
- a mid-range cost with choice of options – where most of your work is done;
- optional extras – profit-laden add-ons.

More examples of adding extras are shown in the table.

Product or service	High-margin added extra
Bicycle hire	Maps
Premixed concrete	Shuttering
Hotel	Flowers and chocolates in room
Car maintenance	Valeting

Remember that you can always discount extras from time to time to create incentives.

9 Online

how to succeed in the virtual world

10 ways to make your website more successful

Almost every enterprise has a website. Many, however, are little more than company brochures pasted into cyberspace. A good website can do much more than simply display your products and services. Here are ten ways you can make your website more successful.

1. **Easy to find** – you want your target audience to find your site. This is as much about the keywords you embed within the site (metatags) as the domain name. Your site needs to contain the words people use to search for what you do. Search engines then find you!

2. **Fast to download** – most people visit a business website for information, not entertainment. Avoid animation and graphics that take a while to download and play. Your visitor probably wants to go straight to the content.

3. **Compatible** – remember that there are several different web browsers. Things that work in Explorer™ may not appear the same in Firefox™. Some web designers forget this and simply design for their favourite web-browsing software.

4. **Accessible** – remember that people with impaired vision may visit your website. Some sites provide an alternative, text-only site as some will find this easier to read. Make sure there is a good contrast between text and background colours. Also make text large enough to read. Remember that when writing text, less can often mean more.

5. **Up to date** – keep adding new content and remove things that become out of date. Adding new content improves your search engine ranking and shows you're busy.

6. **Free stuff** – make sure you have plenty of free stuff for people to read or download. Paradoxically, the more you give away the more people will buy from you.

7. **Collect names** – you want visitor feedback. You also want to build a list of prospects you can keep in touch with. Invite people to register for free newsletters and updates.

8. **Trade links** – add links to other relevant (but not competing) sites and ask others to do the same for you. Make sure that links 'open in a new window' rather than take your visitor away.

9. **Simple** – make sure that the visitor can navigate your site easily. Use simple language, clear signposting and ensure that there's always a navigation toolbar visible.

10. **Silent** – singing avatars or striking music might appeal to you but could really annoy your website visitor. If sound is important to your message, make it optional!

Choosing a web designer

Although it's easy to buy web-building software and attempt to do it yourself, this may not be the best use of your time. When choosing a web designer, look for some key qualities.

- **Creativity** – the ability to interpret and present your message in an interesting way.

- **Common sense** – you want a designer who keeps his/her feet on the ground.

- **Experience** – have they created sites you like? Have they worked in your sector?

- **Content management** – you probably want to be able to add content yourself. Make sure that this is easy for you to do.

- **Evidence of success** – testimonials and a portfolio of good websites are important.

10 ways to network online

One of the internet's greatest strengths is its ability to connect people who otherwise would never find each other. This means you can seek out and find people to work with, buy from, sell to and even have a relationship with. Here are ten ways to network online.

1. **Blog** – there are many websites where you can post blogs. Blogging is rather like keeping an online diary or journal. It's your chance to comment on what's happening. Make your blogs interesting and others will comment or make contact.

2. **Forums** – many websites have forum areas. These enable you to post questions and answer those that others have asked. The best forums are those with a very specific focus. You can pick up good tips and leads from forums read by people in your industry.

3. **User groups** – here you join a closed e-mail 'special interest group' where you can e-mail all members simultaneously. Again, the tighter the focus the more relevant the exchanges. You usually have to apply to join a user group.

4. **Online communities** – there are many online business communities. One of the most popular is *www.ecademy.com*. Online communities enable you to publish your own profile and search for others using keywords. Then you can e-mail to make contact.

5. **Google alerts** – you can set these up from the Google homepage. Once confirmed you will receive an e-mailed link to any new web page that carries your search phrase. Set one up to let you know whenever your name is quoted anywhere on the internet.

6. **RSS** – many good websites provide an RSS feed. This simply means that you can sign up and receive notification whenever the site owner adds new content. Add an RSS feed to your own website and others will be able to see what's new without visiting the site.

7. **Subtle searching** – simply use search engines to find the people you'd like to meet. Then you e-mail them to introduce yourself. Make sure that you make it clear what's in it for them. Don't hassle people – some will simply choose to ignore you, so just accept it.

8. **Diaries and databases** – if you're going to communicate with lots of people, you need to use appropriate software to help you remember what you've agreed to do.

9. **Be receptive** – networking is a two-way process. If people dig you out as part of their online networking, respond politely and be helpful. Help others and others will help you.

10. **Be aware** – in business, as in social networking, everything someone tells you may not be true. Wherever possible look for testimonials and endorsements to back up any claim.

You can waste an awful lot of time networking online. Many people may be keen to chat, but few will be willing to do business with you. Make a clear distinction in your mind between business and social networking. There is a time and a place for both, but when you're working focus on the business opportunities.

Most online networking communities charge a modest monthly subscription. In return you get greater functionality. Some offer access to 'inner circles' of contacts for a higher subscription. You need to be confident that these people will really be useful to you before you sign up.

80:20 rule

Every business textbook talks about the 80:20 rule. The phrase was coined by Pareto and suggests that 80% of the profit comes from 20% of the customers. It also applies to networking in that 20% of your network will deliver 80% of the value you gain. Be selective.

> **GEOFF**
>
> A keen networker and also something of a computer geek, Geoff decided to set up an online business networking community. He set up the website and gave his immediate circle of contacts free access in return for recommending the site to others.
>
> He also sold banner advertising on the site to generate revenue. Take-up was slower than he had hoped for and he became anxious. One day he was rude to a potential advertiser who was being particularly resistant to his invitations to invest. She told people who she networked with that Geoff was not to be trusted.
>
> As is almost always the case, bad news spreads faster than good news. Geoff found it increasingly difficult to recruit subscribers and eventually he gave up.

10 top e-commerce tips

We all dream of a business where you wake up every morning to find that people have been spending money on your website and you have a stack of new orders to fulfil. For some this is a reality. Here are ten top tips to help you do e-commerce.

1. **A good website** – it's obvious but needs stating anyway. People will only spend money via a website that inspires confidence, is clear, professional, accurate and up to date.

2. **Secure payments** – e-commerce means taking credit card payments. These need to be handled securely. Consider getting a proper 'merchant account' from a card provider.

3. **Free tasters** – you need to let your prospects see what it is you are selling. That's why many software companies let you download trial versions with a limited life.

4. **Simple products** – the easier your offer is to understand, the more likely people are to buy. Hotel accommodation, books, music and software are ideal for e-commerce.

5. **Customer feedback** – encourage your customers to post comments and feedback on your website. Positive feedback reassures new customers. Act on negative feedback, thank the person who posted it and then remove it from the site!

6. **Search engine optimisation** – there is a whole science to getting your website higher up the search engine rankings. It's not the only way to attract visitors so spend wisely.

7. **Affiliates** – the more people who are recommending and linking to your site, the more traffic you will get and the more you will sell. Encourage and reward good affiliates.

8. **Google™ advertisements** – you can pay to have your website appear when your chosen 'keywords' are put into the search engine. Google allows you to cap expenditure.

9. **Classified advertising** – remember that you can place small classified ads in printed publications. Such ads need only contain a few words and your website address. Promote an e-commerce website offline as well as online.

10. **Keep in touch** – as with all customers, don't ignore them once they've purchased. Find new things to offer them to keep them spending. Encourage referrals too.

E-commerce opportunities

Almost any business has the opportunity to engage in e-commerce. Not all opportunities are obvious, so here are some you might not have thought of.

- **E-books** – write down all those useful shortcuts you have discovered and add them to your website as downloadable pdf files. Sell them at a low price.

- **Old stock** – create an online 'bargain basement' and use it to sell off stuff you want to get rid of. Include delivery in the price to make it really easy for people to buy.

- **Rare spares** – perhaps you have an interest in classic cars. Find suppliers of those hard-to-get parts and market them online. You sell, they dispatch and you make a profit.

- **Online advice** – if you really know your subject, people will pay to have you answer a question. You might even sell short consultations via online chat or Skype.

- **Photographs** – if you're a keen photographer, sell downloadable images.

> KERRY runs a social enterprise that recycles old computers. She maintains an online stocklist and, once they have been refurbished, sells the recycled equipment to people on limited incomes. To make sure that people can find her website, she has set up computers with internet access at a few community cafes in her town.
>
> Visitors to the cafes can see what stock she has and place their order online. Most pay by debit card. She allows them to spread the cost over three months. Her engineer then delivers and sets up the equipment. Kerry uses the internet to trade locally, not globally.

10 ways to stop your e-mails becoming spam

Every day we are all deluged with unwanted e-mails, or spam. Among them are useful e-mails from friends, family and business contacts. It can be difficult, when the e-mail is from someone you don't know, to decide if it's spam or worth opening. Here are ten ways to stop your selling e-mails being regarded as spam.

1. **The right address** – take the trouble to search your prospect's website and work out the e-mail address of the person you need. Note that e-mails to sales@ or info@ are less likely to be read.

2. **One at a time** – many company spam filters take out e-mails sent through bulk mailing systems. Use online bulk e-mail systems only for those you already know.

3. **The subject line** – writing an appealing subject line is an art form in itself. You need to catch the eye of your prospect, yet you also want to be taken seriously. Treat the subject line as a teaser – composed to draw the reader into the body of the e-mail.

4. **Keep it short** – you want your prospect to read the email and that means keeping it short. Add space between paragraphs to avoid creating a daunting large block of text.

5. **Be specific** – make it very clear what you want the reader to do. If you want them to reply, invite them to 'click reply and tell me . . . '. Note that 'specific' needn't mean blunt!

6. **Use hyperlinks** – if you want your reader to look at a web page, add a hyperlink so they can get there with one click of their mouse. Make it easy and it's more likely to happen.

7. **Be patient** – not everyone will reply straight away and some will not reply at all. If your e-mail hasn't bounced back, you know it's got through. Don't follow up too soon.

8. **Check your spelling** – avoid haste and check your spelling. An effective 'cold call' e-mail might take half an hour to write. Consider composing in Word and pasting into your e-mail. This makes it easier to save for future use.

9. **Avoid flags** – Outlook allows you to flag your e-mail as urgent. Don't do this – use the subject line to explain why you need a quick response.

10. **Keep it clean** – many file servers check e-mails for potentially offensive words and stop them getting through. This could be a problem if you're a baker selling tarts!

E-mail is arguably the greatest advance in commercial communication since the telephone was invented. It enables you to get your message in front of almost anybody. Unlike a phone call, both parties don't need to be there for the message to get through. Here are some other benefits that e-mail offers the entrepreneur:

- **instant** – enabling you to send your message across the world in seconds;

- **attachments** – you can send documents, pictures and more;

- **unobtrusive** – e-mails only interrupt people if they let them, most notice them arrive and then read them later;

- **copies** – you can include several people in one e-mail, although think carefully before copying people in to an e-mail or a reply;

- **cheap** – it costs virtually nothing to send an e-mail.

ALAN runs a company that sells promotional clothing to social and hobby clubs. He finds them on the internet and searches their websites for the name and e-mail address of the secretary. He also looks to see what promotional items they currently provide and what significant events are being planned.

When he e-mails these prospects it is with a well-thought-out, relevant offer. It's not surprising that he wins lots of orders in this way. Research like this almost always pays off.

10 Cash flow

keeping the ship afloat

10 things bank managers like to hear

Bank managers are rarely entrepreneurs. You have to overcome the natural cultural boundary between their nice safe corporate world and your more exciting but risky one. Here are ten things most bank managers like to hear.

1. **I'll risk my money** – no lender will bear all the risk. They want you to risk your money as well. You don't have to risk everything, just enough that it hurts if you lose it.

2. **Sell me more** – bank managers have sales targets. You probably also need life or sickness insurance – buy from your bank and ask what more they can do for you.

3. **Lunch** – treat your bank manager to regular, modest lunches. Encourage open, frank and personal conversation. You want your bank manager to know and like you.

4. **Caution** – banks don't lend to reckless people. Make sure you show some caution.

5. **Good news** – always share good news. Your bank manager will add your letter or perhaps the press cutting you send to your file. It'll help them be more positive if you ever have a problem in the future.

6. **We had a problem** – sort problems and explain how you fixed it. Be honest and open.

7. **Meet my friend** – like anyone in business, banks welcome referrals. Remember that if your bank manager is proud of your business then you will be recommended to others.

8. **We've won** – let's face it, life in a bank can be pretty routine. Enter and win a promotion for a business award and invite your bank manager to the party.

9. **Here are the figures** – in case you've not realised it, bank software calculates all sorts of statistics from the activity on your account. Send them regular management accounts. Add some interpretation to demonstrate you understand what the figures mean.

10. **I want to expand** – you're doing well and everything's hunky-dory. Your bank manager would love to lend you some more money – it's how the banks make money!

Choosing a bank

There has probably never been more choice when it comes to choosing a business bank. As well as the well-known high street names there are many others. Some offer free banking for certain types of business, others charge high fees but offer a more bespoke service.

Too many people complain about banks and their attitude to risk. However, if you've signed your house over as security, it's your fault not theirs! Hermann Hauser, who founded Acorn computers and now runs a venture capital firm, described someone who signs a bank guarantee as 'a fool with a pen'. In other words only sign when you're sure there's no other way.

Here are some things to look for when choosing a bank.

- **Location** – a locally based bank manager will understand the economy and have a good network of contacts. You also want a conveniently close branch for paying in cheques.

- **Accessibility** – internet banking is a must nowadays. You want 24/7 access to your bank balance and the flexibility to make payments online. How good is your bank online?

- **Interest** – you are part of a portfolio of customers handled by your bank manager. Are you very different from the rest? You don't want to be the least important customer.

- **Flexibility** – automatons with lending software on their laptop do not make good bank managers, but some are like that. Seek a manager who appears to be a real person!

- **Direct dial** – don't deal with a bank that won't give you your account manager's phone number. Call centres can be helpful, but at times you simply want to ring your manager.

> TRICIA has a number of sandwich rounds and at the end of the day has a lot of coins to take to the bank. She found banking coins at her high street bank was difficult, in part because of the long queues.
>
> She found another bank that enables her to pay money in at her village post office. This is very convenient and saves her the journey into town. Tricia doesn't have any borrowings and so it was easy to change banks.

10 things your trading terms should include

The small print on the back of your estimates or invoices is just one aspect of trading terms. More important is that you set up deals in a way that makes it easy for your customer to pay you promptly and efficiently. Here are ten things you might try.

1. **Deposits** – if you're buying materials to fulfil an order it's not unreasonable to ask for some money upfront. There's nothing wrong with asking for 30% or more with the order.

2. **Pay on delivery** – why not ask for the balance on delivery? Many web designers, for example, will not post your new site on the internet until you've paid.

3. **Odd numbers** – if you ask for payment in 30 days you'll often wait until the end of the following month. Invoice for payment in 7, 14, 21 or 28 days and you'll get paid faster.

4. **Retainers** – if you do work for someone every month, why not have them set up a regular monthly payment? Work flow may vary but equal regular payments help cash flow.

5. **Maintenance agreements** – charging an annual fee for maintenance means that you can service your customers' equipment when it suits you. This reduces inconvenient emergency call-outs and helps keep your customers loyal. Everyone wins.

6. **Annual increases** – tell customers that you review (increase) your prices annually. This prevents you having to raise the subject because an annual increase is expected.

7. **Incentives** – if referrals are how you win new clients, offer an incentive to reward those who make introductions. Be 'upfront' about this and people will respond.

8. **Prompt payment discount** – add a standard 5% surcharge to your invoice and then show this as a discount for payment-within terms. For some reason this confuses corporate accounts people into settling on time!

9. **Statements** – seen by many as a cop-out from chasing debts, there is no doubt that many companies pay only when they get a statement so send one in good time.

10. **Use the phone** – whatever your terms of business there really is no better way of making sure you get paid on time – polite, pressing phoning prompts payment.

You will notice that the focus of the preceding checklist is on getting payment. Cash is the lifeblood of any business and when you are growing you simply cannot have too much of it. Many people are afraid to ask for the money, choosing instead to send statements and grumpy letters. Here are a few lines you might find useful when asking for your money:

- Your job was one of our biggest this month and your payment is important to our cash flow. Tell me, when can I expect to see the cheque?

- We had to call in a few favours from suppliers to meet your deadline and don't want to keep them waiting for their money. First, though, I need to ask you to pay us. Tell me, when can I expect to see the cheque?

- We're about to invest in a new xyz, which will enable us to do an even better job for you. However, I need to show our bank that we're good at getting the money in. So please, could you send me that cheque?

- Look, I'm working alongside your guys and they got paid last month but I didn't. It's really embarrassing for me. Why have you not paid me yet?

Others will tell you all sorts of gimmicky ways of chasing overdue payments. Avoid trying to be clever – be honest and open instead.

Credit cards

Do not underestimate the value of accepting credit card payments. Many young businesses use them as a line of credit so why not take payments in this way yourself? Although you will pay a commission to your provider (merchant), you will get the money upfront, while your customer may have up to 60 days to pay. Credit cards are also very convenient and you know straight away if the card company refuse the transaction.

Remember that you need one merchant account for sales where the customer is present and another for online trading.

10 things about overdrafts you need to know

Embedded within business folklore is the myth that every business has to have an overdraft. It is true that few can manage growth without but overdrafts are sometimes too easy to obtain and then difficult to reduce. When negotiating your overdraft, be aware of the following ten points.

1. **Guarantee** – overdrafts are nearly always underwritten by your personal guarantee. You're effectively paying a high interest rate to borrow your own money.

2. **Mortgage** – increasing your mortgage on your home can provide cheap money for your business. Your personal liability is no greater than if you had an overdraft.

3. **Fees** – banks charge fees to arrange overdrafts, take guarantees and anything else they can think of. These fees can be significant but are often negotiable.

4. **Not permanent** – overdrafts can be called in by your bank at any time. If worried about your business, banks often wait until your balance is positive and then withdraw the overdraft.

5. **More debt = less profit** – remember that paying interest on loans is eating into your profit. Reduce your borrowings and your profits go up.

6. **It's your business** – remember that your bank is a supplier like any other. Don't let them call the shots – there is probably someone else who will be happy to step into their shoes.

7. **Reports** – most banks demand monthly management accounts when you're in the red. This is good practice, but do make sure you understand them before posting.

8. **Bouncing cheques** – one of the most damaging things any business can do is issue a cheque that bounces. It suggests you're not managing your cash flow and leads to loss of trust.

9. **Cash-flow forecasts** – before borrowing, work out when your cash flow will render the overdraft unnecessary. If it doesn't, there may be a problem with your costings.

10. **Insurance** – many banks sell you insurance so that the overdraft is repaid if you die or get very sick. This insurance can be surprisingly expensive – it's another one of those unexpected costs.

Of course, overdrafts are not all bad news and most of us have them from time to time. The art is not thinking of an overdraft as being essential, especially when you start your business. Too many people use their overdraft to pay themselves a salary when, frankly, they'd be better living more frugally and leaving the money in the bank. Overdrafts should be used to:

- provide working capital for the everyday trading you do;
- give you a little flexibility to cope with the unexpected.

Some of our case study businesses found ways to start their business without an overdraft:

- Malcolm used contract labour rather than employing a full time team;
- Simon worked as a postman every morning, starting in his own office at 10 am;
- Raymond drove a lorry, doing business via his mobile phone along the way.

10 ways to finance your business

Overdrafts are good ways to fund your cash flow. To establish your business, or perhaps buy plant and equipment, you may need long-term finance. There are several places you can look but not all of them are obvious. Here are ten you might consider.

1. **Credit cards** – people starting consultancy or design businesses always seem the most skilled at moving debt around their credit cards, taking advantage of interest-free introductory offers. It's probably not the best way to find cash but is the quickest!

2. **Bank loan** – always secured against your assets, but with planned repayments. Unlike an overdraft, a loan cannot be called in unless you default on the repayments.

3. **Prince's Trust** – if you're under 30 and starting out this trust might lend you money when everyone else says no. The trust also finds you a business mentor.

4. **Old policies** – check out those long-term insurance policies you fund. You might be able to borrow against them at a low interest rate. Ask your insurance broker.

5. **Mortgage** – release some equity from the family home. It's cheap, but may be unsettling for those you love and live with. Be sure to pay it back!

6. **Small Firms Loan Guarantee scheme** – if you have not got the assets to secure a bank loan, sometimes you can get one of these. The loan is underwritten by the Government who give the bank 85% of the cash if your business fails.

7. **Sell and lease back** – you can usually sell and lease back business assets such as machinery and vehicles. This frees up hard cash to fund business growth.

8. **Factoring** – by putting your debtors with a factor, who pays you straight away (less a fee and interest) and then collects your debts, you gain around one month's turnover.

9. **Public sector** – councils and the many other public sector organisations that exist to drive economic regeneration and growth often offer loan schemes. Check them out.

10. **Make sure** – before burdening your business with debt make sure that it really is necessary. Work out how you'd get there without the loan. Is this a better route?

Top tip

If you jointly own your home and your partner refuses to offer it as security for a bank loan, you may well qualify for support under the Small Firms Loan Guarantee scheme. The reason is that the asset is jointly owned and both owners need to consent to it being used as security. Encouraging your partner to refuse to allow you to borrow against the family home can make it less problematical if your business partner has no assets against which to secure business borrowing. Exposure to different degrees of financial risk can damage the relationships between business partners when things get tough.

Arranging bank loans

Too many people use overdraft finance to cover long-term debt. That's because it's often easier to increase the overdraft than to arrange a loan. Here are a few things you need to have in place before applying for a loan:

- your business plan should be up to date;
- cash-flow projections that show the future with and without the loan;
- an optimistic and a pessimistic forecast;
- a 'get-out route' if the investment doesn't work for both you and the lender;
- evidence of how others have profited from doing what you're planning to do.

10 ways to avoid running out of cash

Fast-growing businesses sometimes run out of cash. It's one of the major causes of business collapse. Quite simply, as turnover grows so does demand for working capital – you're really busy, selling lots, but run out of money. Here are ten ways to avoid it.

1. **See it coming** – if you use a spreadsheet to forecast your cash flow accurately, you will see the danger signs a few months in advance. Act early and you can turn it round.

2. **Chase your debts** – if you are busy then making sure you get paid often slips down the priority list. Always chase your debts and get the cash in.

3. **Stall suppliers** – everyone starts paying late when things get tight. However, clever people discuss the issue with their supplier first because then they're less likely to worry.

4. **Focus on the profitable** – if you have unprofitable activities or products, consider ditching them. Too often we hang on to the stuff we should really let go.

5. **Tell the bank** – as long as you have a plan and can show that you're on top of the situation, the bank will often provide short-term additional finance.

6. **Shift stock** – look around and see if you're carrying stock you could quickly liquidate. Sell the stuff you no longer need. Take junk to an auction and get rid of it. Get tidy.

7. **Salary holiday** – stopping your own pay for a month or so shows those around you that you are committed to winning. When things are fixed take a bonus!

8. **VAT** – talk to those you pay taxes to and explain the situation. They'll often negotiate a deferred payment deal to help you out. Always ask first. They get angry if you don't!

9. **Prepayments** – watch out that you're not using prepayments for future work to pay for supplies used to meet today's orders. This might indicate that you're insolvent.

10. **Get tough** – you need to squeeze money back into your cash flow. Maybe there are things you could actually do without? Batten down the hatches and chuck excess expense overboard.

Banks will tell you that when cash gets tight it's because the business owner:

- has no proper cash-flow forecast so is caught out when it's almost too late;
- takes it personally and goes into denial, ignoring the risk and getting angry;
- blames others and fails to recognise the need to change the way they operate;
- panics and becomes less efficient, risking customer and supplier goodwill;
- gives up the fight before they've even started.

The art is to see danger coming and trim your business to weather the storm. You need to prepare a cash-flow forecast that allows you to see the impact on your overdraft of sharp increases in sales, delays in customer payments and rises in your business costs. Many business-support organisations and banks can give you prepared spreadsheets into which you simply enter your own figures. These are great – they also form a checklist for the things you might otherwise overlook. People often forget to include in their cash-flow forecasting:

- VAT payments, due quarterly;
- VAT collected on sales;
- employer's National Insurance;
- quarterly payments, for example machinery leases;
- repayments of existing loans.

11 Costs

how to avoid bad debts and pay suppliers

10 things all good customers have in common

It may seem obvious, but there is more to a good customer than initially meets the eye. Here then are ten traits which combine to make the perfect customer.

1. **Trust** – the best thing customers can give you is their trust. In return, you must be honest and trust them too. If they pay without quibble, your invoicing must be scrupulously fair.

2. **Tolerance** – a sure sign of a good trading relationship is where problems are resolved amicably. Tolerance is about taking the long-term view – it is not about conflict.

3. **Potential** – a customer business that is growing can give you lots more – you will literally grow together.

4. **Status** – if you work with the best you will be considered the best. If you work with losers your life will be marked by bumps and struggles.

5. **Friends** – the well-networked customer will pass you around. Impress customers with a good network and you have your passport to that network.

6. **Good address** – customers from affluent neighbourhoods will often buy more from you. They are also likely to give you high-quality referrals.

7. **Vision** – if your customers know where they are going, they define your role in their plans. You can work together to develop new ideas. You can win long-term contracts.

8. **Faults** – when you see customers' faults, you've really got to know them well. If you can fix faults without being asked then you are indispensable.

9. **Fun** – Plato said you could learn more from an hour's play than a year's conversation. Have fun with your customers. Play to win!

10. **Cash** – it may seem obvious but some really nice firms lead their marketplace and yet run on fresh air. However good a business, it can only help you if fully funded.

Of course, in an ideal world your customers will find you. This is more certainly the case if you have a retail business that relies on passing trade. However much your customer group is self-selecting, it's good to encourage the people you want to do business with and discourage those who make you less profit. This chapter is about managing your costs and so we need to focus on how you can make more profit from each customer. Here are some ways to encourage existing customers to make you more profit by costing you less:

- **take fewer, larger consignments** – it's usually cheaper to make up bigger orders;

- **simplify your range** – the more different things you make or do, the more stock you need and the more complex your organisation. Cut out marginal activities;

- **let go of the small customers** you've outgrown and spend the time you save winning new bigger ones.

10 things all good suppliers have in common

Your suppliers are as important to you as your customers. This is true if you are a manufacturer buying components or a consultancy with freelance associates. Your best suppliers will be those that offer you these ten qualities.

1. **Reliability** – your reputation hangs on your suppliers' ability to meet your needs. If they let you down, you end up letting your customers down. Make sure they're reliable.

2. **Tolerance** – you are unlikely to be perfect either! Good suppliers tolerate those panic phone calls and try their best to get you out of a muddle – even when it's self-inflicted.

3. **Potential** – you want suppliers who can grow with you. They should share your ambition and be prepared to invest in keeping up with you. Notice if you outgrow a supplier.

4. **Quality** – wherever possible you need to buy the best. Don't encourage suppliers to cut corners to reduce costs. You will be the loser. Charge more yourself instead.

5. **Stability** – there are lots of factors that can destablilise a supplier. Take an interest in their aspirations, achievements and challenges. You want to avoid nasty surprises.

6. **Good suppliers** – your supplier buys as well as sells. How good are their suppliers?

7. **Deep pockets** – when your cash flow hiccups, the first people you lean on for credit are your suppliers. Can they support you in times of trouble?

8. **Great people** – any business is only as good as its people. Good suppliers have motivated, able, enthusiastic people. Get to know the people who work on your behalf.

9. **Enquiring minds** – nothing stays the same for long. You want suppliers that are constantly seeking improvement. Are yours exploring new and innovative ideas?

10. **Fun** – you will get more from your suppliers if their people socialise with your people. Why not challenge them to five-a-side football?

Finding good suppliers is as important as finding good customers. In fact, to enjoy success you need both. Here are some places you might look:

- trade journals;
- industry exhibitions;
- local business networks;
- the internet;
- competitors' products (to identify component suppliers);
- professional and trade organisations (to identify associates);
- friends in similar businesses to yourself – ask for recommendations;
- foreign trade missions able to introduce overseas suppliers;
- university research teams working in your industry area;
- newspapers reporting business achievement.

You will be a better customer to your suppliers if you:

- agree annual targets and work together to achieve them;
- confirm orders in writing and make them clear and specific;
- don't blame your suppliers for your own mistakes;
- pay when you say you will, even if it's late;
- give constructive feedback to encourage innovation.

JULIAN and his brother Lincoln are printers. Their firm was established by their great-grandfather and they are very much part of their local business scene. Not content to rest on the laurels of previous generations, they have invested substantially in premises, plant and people.

Julian is never complacent about his role as a supplier. His quotations are delivered quickly, the customer always knows where their job is in the production process and he watches his rivals all the time.

Keen on water sports, Julian invested in equipment for his speedboat that enables even novice water-skiers to succeed. Most summer weekends he is out with customers teaching them a new skill and building the bond of trust between them.

10 taxes you need to know about

Nobody likes paying taxes but they are a cost to your business all the same. It often pays to take professional advice to minimise your tax liability. Remember though that your business should focus on maximising your profit opportunity, not reducing your tax burden. Note too that there is a fine line to tread between the good practice of 'tax avoidance' and the illegal practice of 'tax evasion'. Here are ten tax basics you may not yet know.

1. **Income tax** – is what you have probably paid at some point as an employee. It is deducted from your pay and sent to HMRC on your behalf. As an employer you do the deducting and sending. It's rarely worth calculating yourself – use a bureau service instead. If you run a limited company you will pay income tax too.

2. **Self-assessment** – is what you do as a self-employed person or partner in an unincorporated firm. You then pay your 'income' tax in two lumps, in January and July. Your accountant can help you to complete the forms, or you can do it yourself online.

3. **National Insurance** – this tax affects both employees and employers. Employers pay this to HMRC. Never be tempted to make them wait for tax payments – tax officials can get very angry very quickly!

4. **VAT** – if your sales exceed a certain threshold you have to register for and charge VAT. This can be a real problem if you sell to consumers who cannot reclaim the tax as a business might. However, once registered you can reclaim VAT that others charge you.

5. **Business rates** – this tax is charged on business premises and collected by the local authority. Some landlords include it in the rent.

6. **Corporation tax** – limited companies and PLCs pay this. It is levied on profits and can be reduced by investing in equipment that can be depreciated against the tax liability.

7. **Cars and vans** – if you are a director or employee of your business and the business runs your car, you will be taxed on it as a 'benefit in kind'. If you are self-employed the deal is usually better. If you use your own car in your business you can pay yourself certain tax-free allowances towards the running costs.

8. **Expenses** – if you incur expenses, say for rail travel in connection with your business, you can pay yourself back. You need to keep receipts and not claim personal expenses.

9. **Overseas** – when you buy or sell outside the UK, particularly outside Europe, you may incur additional tax liabilities. Your local Chamber of Commerce can advise you.

10. **Cash** – tax officials know what kinds of business have the most cash transactions. They can calculate what your sales should be from your purchases. Don't pocket the cash!

Accountants

The cost of a good accountant is almost always recouped by the amount of tax saved. Many allow you to pay them in monthly instalments so you hardly notice the annual bill when it arrives. Choosing the right accountant for you and your business is really important. Here are some pointers to help you find the best for you.

- **Recommendation** – ask people you like and respect who they use and why.

- **Local** – it's usually best to choose someone nearby because it's easier to visit each other.

- **Appropriate** – choose an accountant who works with businesses of the size you plan to be. This makes it less likely you'll outgrow your accountant.

- **Values** – we all have different values, attitudes and opinions. Choosing an accountant that thinks the way that you do will help you both get on.

- **Price** – don't choose on price because cheapest isn't always best.

10 ways to collect an overdue payment

Getting the money in is vital. Sometimes you need to chase overdue payments. Here are ten effective ways to get paid.

1. **Ask** – obvious though it sounds, many people are reluctant to ask for money choosing instead to write or send statements. Avoid using euphemisms – just ask for the cheque.

2. **Statements** – some companies only pay when a statement arrives. Send statements.

3. **Know who** – establish rapport with the person who actually handles each significant customer's payments. Get to know them and make sure they put you at the top of the pile.

4. **Pop in** – if you sell to the public it's always best to get paid when you've finished the job. If you find yourself waiting for payment, call round and ask for a cheque.

5. **Ring at home** – Companies House can tell you where directors live. If you've been unable to get through to them at work, look up their home phone number and ring them in the evening. Of course it's obtrusive but that's why it works!

6. **Solicitors** – many law firms offer a debt-chasing service. These can be effective.

7. **Avoid emotion** – however angry or let down you feel, don't lose your temper. It doesn't help matters, in fact it can make them worse.

8. **Small claim** – it is a simple, but lengthy, process to take a customer to the Small Claims Court. You can do it yourself but be prepared to argue your case in front of a judge.

9. **Garnishee order** – if the customer's going bust, getting a garnishee order from the court means you get paid directly by their customers. Great if what you sold them has been sold on.

10. **Why bother?** – it's the small debts that always annoy. Every month they take time, cause anxiety and simply sit on your books. Write off small bad debts and move on.

Managing customer expectations is the key to getting paid. A gentle reminder ahead of the due date can make sure your invoice filters through to the accounts team.

If you sell one-off products or services then you need to spell out to the customer what your trading terms are. This is best done when the order is placed and confirmed.

When asking for payment:

- have the figures to hand and make sure they're accurate;

- remain polite and objective;

- if there's a problem with your product or service, apologise and fix it, then ask again;

- listen sympathetically to the reasons for late payment you hear;

- be realistic and compassionate if the reason for delay is genuine.

ARTHUR had a courier business and he asked a design company he worked for to produce a company brochure for him. He wanted the brochure because business was difficult. He could not pay for the work done and shared his business problems with his customer.

The design company happened to do work for a mortgage broker who helped Arthur remortgage his house to inject more capital into his business. The brochure and extra cash gave Arthur's business the momentum it needed. He now employs 15 people.

Sometimes you have to be very creative when collecting overdue debts.

12 Premises

where to work and how to make it work

10 good reasons to work from home

Working from home is incredibly convenient. If you're starting your business it's also the place you have already. Of course you need some space and there may be distractions, but there are lots of good reasons for working from home. Here are ten of them.

1. **Cheap** – the money you save by not renting an office can be invested instead in technology, marketing and other things that build your business.

2. **Commuting** – travelling a few feet to the office each day can make a refreshing change after years of catching the 07.30 train. You can work longer hours in shorter days.

3. **Convenient** – if you are the creative type, or just like to work at odd times, working from home means you can go into the office whenever you want.

4. **Childcare** – while something of a two-edged sword, working from home makes childcare a lot easier. It's also easier to fit your work around school sports day!

5. **Coffee shops** – even those with an office frequently choose to meet clients in a mutually convenient coffee shop. Use coffee shops to meet people. Most also have wireless broadband so you can take your laptop and work between meetings.

6. **Crises** – life is littered with domestic crises. It can be useful to be at home working during the day, even if it's only to let the plumber in when he calls to mend a tap.

7. **Comfortable** – OK, you need to create a work-like environment, but when you're having a day at the office you can dress down as far as you like.

8. **Colleagues** – you will undoubtedly have people who work with you either regularly or on a project basis. You can use 'voice over internet' packages, such as Skype, to hold teleconferences for free. You can also videoconference over the internet.

9. **Environment** – if you like to listen to music you can. You can also have the windows open in winter or the heating on in summer. You can create the environment you want.

10. **Colds** – you know when someone starts sneezing in an open-plan office? Soon everyone's reaching for the tissues. Working from home is healthy too!

Some people, however, really do need the discipline of working alongside others. They find it difficult to apply themselves at home, or home simply does not afford the space. If this is you, then consider some alternatives.

- **Sharing** – a rented office with someone else. You don't have to be working in the same business, just someone like you who wants a work buddy.

- **Hot desk** – many business centres now provide hot-desking. This enables you to pay for space only when you're using it. Business centres usually also have meeting rooms.

- **Empty office** – sometimes your best customer will happily give you work-space in exchange for the convenience of having you on site. This works well for consultants.

- **Clubs** – particularly in London, there are many clubs and organisations that provide their members with places to meet, work and do business.

If you do work from home you must remember:

- to make sure you have office contents and public liability insurance;
- that you can reclaim some of the household bills against your profits;
- that it makes sense to tell your neighbours if you're going to have lots of visitors;
- your workspace should not be exclusively for work – this can have tax repercussions;
- to have a separate work phone number so that you can answer it professionally.

PAUL set up a warehousing and distribution business. His first customer wanted to outsource this aspect of their work and had warehousing they no longer needed. Paul took over the warehouse with rent being deducted from his monthly invoice to them.
He then had space to store products on behalf of his other customers.

10 ways to look bigger than you are

Sometimes, small is beautiful. However, when you're pitching for really big contracts it often pays to look bigger than you are. This avoids the customers' very natural worry that you will not have the capaicity to deliver. Here are ten ways to look bigger than you are.

1. **Good address** – if you work from home, adapt your address to make it look more like a business address. Drop the house number and avoid PO boxes. Become XYZ House.

2. **Phone answering** – have your phone diverted to a call-answering service when you are out. This is more reliable and more professional than forwarding calls to your mobile.

3. **Share facilities** – if you rent part of a building and another tenant has a better meeting room than you, borrow it when important clients visit.

4. **Website** – your virtual business environment should always be a few steps ahead of reality. Websites are cheaper than premises and are usually visited more often.

5. **Nice car** – however hard we try not to, we all judge our visitors by the cars they drive. If you usually go to your customers make sure you drive a nice car. Also keep it clean!

6. **Think big** – your words will give you away. Make sure you think, talk and walk big. Always talk your business up and remember that your competitors probably do the same.

7. **Associates** – a network of associates gives you manpower when you need it, and no overhead costs when you don't. Create a network of freelancers able to help.

8. **Branding** – if subcontractors visit your customers, perhaps as service engineers or to make deliveries, have your livery on their vehicles. Make it a condition of contract.

9. **Proactive** – big businesses usually appear to be efficient. Investing in client management software and keeping in touch with your prospects creates that successful, large image.

10. **Bluff** – in reality big firms can be less efficient than small ones. The art is to say 'yes, no problem' to the customer and then sort out how to make it happen later. We all 'wing it'!

Often the need to appear larger than you are, or perhaps be based in more prestigious premises, is more of a worry to you than to your customer. Remember that most companies in the UK are small, employing fewer than five people. If you need reassuring that it's good to be small here are some benefits to consider.

- **Low overheads** – small businesses have small overheads and can often charge less.

- **Customers are valued** – with a small company each customer is important.

- **Adaptability** – unrestrained by the inflexible systems, culture and tradition of big business, small firms are usually willing and able to adapt to deliver exactly what you want.

- **Accountability** – small firms don't have lots of different departments. Everyone is accountable for what is done for the customer. There's no passing the buck.

- **Transparency** – with a small business what the customer sees is what they get.

10 premises traps and how to avoid them

If your business is growing then it will inevitably need premises. Unless you are able to buy a place you will need to rent or lease premises. Here are ten things to look out for.

1. **Long lease** – most leases are short these days. You want to be able to move on if you outgrow the place – it's usually best to avoid long leases.

2. **Break clauses** – good leases have break clauses. These are opportunities to 'break' the lease and move out.

3. **Repairs** – check if you are to be liable for repairs. Repairs can be expensive!

4. **Rates** – it's easy to forget that you'll also be paying local authority business rates. These can be high, particularly for retail premises.

5. **Service charge** – if you're in a shared complex you will probably be asked to pay a service charge to cover things like maintenance, cleaning and heating.

6. **Power** – many landlords individually meter and mark-up electricity, gas and telephony. Compare the rates with what you pay now. How much more will it be costing you?

7. **What's next door?** – what nearby businesses do will make a difference. It's difficult, for example, to run a call centre with a foundry in the next unit.

8. **Restrictions** – sometimes your lease or agreement will exclude some activities you might want to carry out. Check the small print carefully.

9. **Security** – insuring your enterprise in business premises can be expensive. You will probably need an alarm system connected to a control centre – this costs too.

10. **Parking** – your staff might all come to work by bus, but if your customers drive to you where will they park? Is there enough parking for your team as well?

Most landlords use a standard lease that is simply adapted for each unit. Leases are legal documents and there are often fees associated with setting one up. It is always wise to take independent legal advice before signing a lease for premises.

A place of your own

While it is often prudent to rent business premises and focus your own investment on the operational side of your venture, buying a place of your own makes sense in some circumstances. What's more, buying premises can be easier than you might think. It is possible, in some circumstances, for the owners of a business to pool their pension funds and use this as the deposit for a commercial property with the remainder being covered by a commercial mortgage. The mortgage payments are funded from the monthly rent you pay. When you retire, the property forms part of your pension scheme. Pension legislation is complex and changes frequently so take independent advice. However, the principle of using the rent you would otherwise pay to a landlord to fund your pension is worth considering, particularly if you expect to remain at the same location for many years.

Redundant buildings

To encourage you to restore a derelict building, grants are often available to contribute to the capital costs. Finding the right place can give you the chance to develop the buildings as your business grows, funding the development from cash flow.

GEORGE, who has a software company, purchased a derelict farmhouse and buildings. A grant helped with the conversion costs and, because he was going to live there too, he obtained a homeowner's mortgage, which costs less than a commercial loan. His company pays him rent for the space it occupies and this more than covers the mortgage.

13 People

how to hire and manage good people

10 questions to ask when recruiting

Without good people your business cannot grow. Recruiting the right people is vital to your continued success. Here are ten questions you might like to ask potential recruits when interviewing.

1. **Talk me through your career to date** – listen for and explore any gaps.

2. **What have been your greatest achievements?** – find out the highlights of the candidate's career so far. What they are proudest of having done and why?

3. **What has been your biggest mistake?** – making mistakes is how we all learn so the more the better, within reason! Assure candidates that this is not a trick question!

4. **How do you want to be spending your time in three years' time?** – reveals where they see their career going. Do you want an ambitious person or someone to stick at one job?

5. **What appeals most about working here?** – this question reveals how much research they've done for the interview. Good candidates will have done their homework.

6. **What appeals least about working here?** – do they trust you enough to tell you? If not, have you failed to make them feel at ease with you? You will learn from honest answers.

7. **If you won £1m tomorrow how would you spend it?** – good to know what your candidate dreams of doing. Don't be surprised if they say they'd still work – many would.

8. **What is the question you would most like me to ask you?** – if you've established a good rapport the answer to this may reveal their concerns about your organisation.

9. **What is the question you hope I don't ask?** – again, this encourages them to reveal fears and doubts. Respect them for what they are and reassure them.

10. **When I'm making my decision, what do you most want me to remember about you?** – encourages them to summarise the key benefits they bring.

Before you seek people to interview:

*   define the job and how it fits within the organisation's structure – write a job description;

- • check out what other employers offer for the same job – talk to trade bodies;
- .work out the total cost of hiring someone – include everything, even training;
- calculate the financial return on this investment – make sure they'll make you money.

You can find potential new employees by:

- advertising in local, national or trade publications;
- putting a sign outside your door;
- asking existing employees who they know;
- asking customers who they know;
- networking;
- using a recruitment agency.

Job advertisements should always contain:

- the job title;
- the salary range and benefits;
- your contact details;
- a promise of confidentiality;
- positive reasons for joining your firm.

When interviewing:

- do not face the candidate over a desk – create a more friendly environment instead;
- listen more than you talk – this is vital if you are to understand the candidate fully;
- take notes and consider taking a photograph to help you remember who was who;
- smile – an interview can be daunting for both of you so keep it light and informal;
- offer to reimburse travel expenses;
- say thank you at the end and ask for feedback on the interview.

10 positive ways to keep your employees happy

Employment legislation exists to protect both employees and employers. However, it usually only becomes an issue when things go wrong. Here are ten ways to get it right.

1. **Be nice** – 99.99% of people are decent, honest and reliable. Treat your people well and they will treat you well too. Most legislation is only relevant when things go wrong.

2. **Give a contract** – get a solicitor to draft an employment contract that protects both you and your staff. Encourage the use of friendly language. Adapt for each new employee.

3. **Be specific** – tell people what you want them to do and make sure they understand.

4. **Train** – invest in training so that people can do their jobs confidently and feel developed.

5. **Listen** – create opportunities or procedures so that your people can tell you what they think could be different or better. Encourage them to be innovative.

6. **Comply** – make sure that your workplace is safe, comfortable and clean. Make it clear that you want things done properly and that corners should not be cut.

7. **Consult** – take advice where you need to. Borrow good ideas that have worked elsewhere.

8. **Encourage volunteering** – encourage people to spend time helping others.

9. **Incentives** – offer the team incentives if agreed targets are achieved. If you're in the voluntary/community sector then make the reward something other than money.

10. **Borrow their eyes** – it's different being the boss. Take a look at life through your employees' eyes. Change the things you see and don't like.

Employees are usually employees because they do not want to take big risks, and they enjoy the security of a regular pay cheque. They tend not to be comfortable taking the lead either so you need to demonstrate clear leadership.

Whatever your organisation does you, as the boss, have different motives for working from those you employ and manage. Remember that many people find it difficult to imagine what it would be like to be in charge. It's simply not something they'd ever consider doing.

What can go wrong?

People will always surprise you, none more so than those you employ. They can delight, amaze and impress. They also have the ability to cause you a lot of trouble. Usually, though, when things go wrong it's as much the fault of the employer as the employee. Legislation exists to protect the employee from abuse and discrimination. It can trip you up if you fail to stick to the rules. Here are some areas where it's best to tread carefully.

- **Disability** – it is illegal to discriminate against people with disabilities, providing they have the skills and experience to do the job. Remember that people can have physical, mental or learning disabilities. You can sometimes get grants towards adapting the workplace, or providing additional support, for an employee with a disability.

- **Equality** -- everyone is equally entitled to express their individuality. Be careful you cannot be found to have discriminated on grounds of faith, gender or sexuality.

- **Babies** – steer well clear of asking questions of your female employees about their plans to have babies. It can land you in very hot water if they claim that you have discriminated.

- **Performance** – if someone is not performing you need to follow the correct procedures for dealing with this. Take advice before acting and try to find out what is behind the problem. Make sure you're not simply expecting more than is reasonable.

- **Communication** – most workplace problems are the result of poor communication. The people who work for you are not stupid – they can work out what's happening. Keep employees in the picture so that they can feel part of what is going on.

10 things that will make you a better boss

It's almost a cliché but it can never be said too many times – your people are the biggest investment your business will ever make. For most businesses the wage bill is the biggest monthly cost. Here are ten ways you can become a better boss.

1. **Big ears** – good bosses not only listen, they take a genuine interest in their staff.

2. **Long legs** – be seen to be interested and involved. Walk around the place – be seen.

3. **White teeth** – smiling bosses make people happy – don't be grumpy as it can spread!

4. **Dirty hands** – in most small businesses there are always grotty jobs like unblocking toilets. Show that you're prepared to get your hands dirty.

5. **An open door** – at times you need to be left alone. Not everything you do can be shared, but being accessible is the best way to know what's happening.

6. **Clear vision** – people follow leaders who know where they're going and who don't falter.

7. **Tongue control** – emotional responses, such as shouting and ranting, have their place but not if it means humiliating your staff. Sometimes it's best to hold your tongue.

8. **Strong stomach** – remember how officers led their men to certain death in the battles of the Somme? Like them, if it's getting tough, you must not let your fear show.

9. **Firm hand** – you are the boss. You are expected to make unpopular decisions where necessary and to be firm with those who don't pull their weight. Don't be too soft.

10. **Love** – we are all human. We all like to be loved – good bosses show true love and compassion. Being heartless and brutal will not make you rich.

It may sound idealistic to be a touchy-feely caring employer when the bank has a charge over your house and things aren't going as well as you'd hoped. However, being a great boss need not cost you the earth. Here are a few very affordable ways to make your business a great place to work.

- **Soft loo paper** – pay the extra few pence for the good stuff. Also make sure toilets are clean and in good working order.

- **Graffiti board** – why not create places for your staff to have their say, free from criticism or retribution?

- **Good tools** – usually the best tools cost less than the wrong tools and waste less time.

- **Party** – investing £10 per head in a visit to the pub after work on Friday can deliver hundreds of pounds worth of extra work next week.

- **Surprises** – we all like nice surprises, for example ice cream on a hot day.

CLIVE

When Clive took over a company he had once worked for, he was determined to be a better employer than his boss had been. When he'd worked there before, cash had been tight and improvisation part of everyday life. Every piece of equipment had been faulty.

Although he reorganised the workshops, improving the workflow and buying new equipment, one of the most popular improvements was the £70 microwave oven installed in the freshly painted staffroom. It meant people could have a hot lunch.

10 ways to delegate and know the job will get done

Letting go of the stuff you used to do is the only way to grow your organisation. As headcount rises your job becomes more strategic, with others doing the day-to-day tasks. Remember you may be able to do their jobs, but they can't do yours. Here are ten tips on delegation.

1. **Explain** – tell people exactly what you want done and why it's important.

2. **Invest** – spend time and money making sure everyone has the right equipment and skills.

3. **Encourage innovation** – the way you used to do it may not be the best way today. Encouraging others might find new and better ways to get things done.

4. **Allow mistakes** – it won't always be right first time. Accept a few mistakes.

5. **Allow routine** – let operational things become a series of routines. You might prefer every day to be an adventure but your staff probably would not.

6. **Empower** – make people responsible – give them scope to be flexible and to adapt. Let them make the job their own.

7. **Don't interfere** – having delegated, the worst thing you can do is interfere. Wait to be asked for help. Create systems that enable you to monitor what's going on.

8. **'Morning prayers'** – lots of teams start the day with a twenty-minute briefing. It allows everyone to know what's new, different or urgent. Do it standing up. Make it fun.

9. **Explore new things** – if you can delegate all your tasks you are not redundant. You now have time to dedicate to planning for the future.

10. **Celebrate** – create milestones and celebrate with the team when they are reached.

Delegating in a social enterprise

In general, people who work for social enterprises are more passionate, idealistic and enthusiastic than workers in the 'for profit' sector. However, this can make them prone to deciding that the vision they have for the organisation is better than yours. You can manage this by:

- involving your team in developing the strategy you want them to follow;
- collecting and then discussing feedback from customers and service users;
- accepting that you won't be right all the time – don't suppress good ideas;
- helping everyone to stay abreast of the current debates in your sector.

Getting strategic

So you've delegated and now have more time on your hands. Here are five things you could do tomorrow that you didn't have time to consider today.

- **Clear** your desk of clutter, put your feet up and reread your business plan.
- **Visit** your five best customers and find out how you could both be more successful.
- **Research** and try to understand your competitors better.
- **Take time out**, relax and think about where you want your organisation to go.
- **Book a surprise** weekend away and treat your family to your attention.

14 Motivation

adding momentum and magic

10 ways to motivate yourself

It's your business, your future and your opportunity. However, from time to time your enthusiasm wanes and, being the boss, there's no one else to pick you up and get you going again. Here are ten ways to motivate yourself.

1. **Read the plan** – dig out your business plan and remind yourself why it is you're doing all this. We all lose sight of the vision from time to time – bring it back to life.

2. **Break it down** – at times challenges can seem overwhelming. Break them down into smaller tasks and conquer them one at a time. Take it one step at a time.

3. **Plot your course** – line up those 'bite-sized' challenges and join them together. See how they lead you closer towards your goal.

4. **Writing on the wall** – put key performance measures on the wall where you can see them. Make it visual – graphs are better than words.

5. **Involve others** – if you employ people, it has to be their challenge too. Motivating others by sharing the tasks will also motivate you.

6. **Check your champions** – when you're feeling down others always seem to be far more successful. Check where they were when at your stage – you might actually be ahead.

7. **Open the window** – are you too close to the job? Open the window, breathe in fresh air and marvel at the natural world. Put work into perspective.

8. **Say no** – if you're feeling demotivated you need some time to yourself. Clear space in your diary and focus on your needs rather than those of the people around you.

9. **Check your health** – are you losing motivation because you are ill or unfit? Check it out and do something about it. It's easier to be motivated when you're fit and well.

10. **Celebrate** – when you hit a target have a party. Mark each success along the way.

One of the reasons why new entrepreneurs struggle with self-motivation is that they are making the transition from manager. Many people leave a management job to go it alone. Entrepreneurs are different and, while good managers can make good entrepreneurs, they need to recognise the need for and to develop new skills. Here are some key differences.

Entrepreneurs	Managers
Create ideas and develop strategy	Translate strategy into action
Are rarely team players	Achieve through others
Prefer doing new things	Measure and improve performance
Just do it	Assess risks and plan to reduce them

Many entrepreneurs encounter a growth barrier when the staff totals around 15. At this point the entrepreneurial founder has three options:

- learn to become a manager (again) and suppress the entrepreneurial instinct;

- hire a professional manager to run the business so that the owner can continue to explore;

- sell.

ALAN started his business when his boss made him redundant. He is not a natural entrepreneur but was spurred into self-employment by the loss of his job. He finds it difficult to stay motivated, particularly now the feelings of anger about redundancy have faded.

Gadgets have always excited Alan and now that he has his own firm he can indulge his passion for technology. What he has learned to do is to work out what gadget he wants to buy and then promise it himself as a reward for achieving a challenging business goal.

10 ways to motivate employees

As well as formal goal-setting, regular appraisals and training plans you also need the people who work for you to really want to succeed. Remember it's your business not theirs – there is much more to motivating people than just regular pay cheques. Consider adopting some of the following for your staff.

1. **Bright and light** – banish brown paint and dirty windows. Make the work environment light and comfortable. Why not some comfy sofas for meetings instead of hard chairs?

2. **Keep it clean** – nobody likes to come in to work and find the bin full and the toilets smelly. Invest in a good cleaner and everyone will be much happier.

3. **Be flexible** – why not let people start early and go home early in the summer? Consider an annualised-hours scheme which makes it easier to manage both your workload and their work–life balance.

4. **Celebrate together** – birthdays, new business wins and even Fridays can be good reasons to buy cakes for everyone.

5. **Nice drinks** – it's amazing how awful some cheap coffees taste. Treat people to decent drinks at work and don't make them pay. Ask people what they'd like and stock it.

6. **Create competitions** – lighthearted prizes for hitting targets make winning part of your workplace culture. Design some competitions to be won by junior team members.

7. **Organise outings** – do your staff work in the same place all the time? Take them out to meet customers, to hear relevant speakers and see things that will shape their work.

8. **Sports** – encourage fitness by subsidising gym membership. People who are fit tend to enjoy better health and take less sick leave. Gym membership can be a good investment.

9. **Support their cause** – everyone has a cause they feel strongly about. Your staff will welcome you taking an interest, and perhaps even helping them out.

10. **Offer alternatives** – remember that while some are extrovert others are shy. Be careful not to create a culture where people feel obliged to take part in things they'd rather miss.

Rewards packages

Everyone is different. Many large employers provide a flexible range of employment benefits from which employees can select. This enables people to be rewarded in the way that best suits their individual needs. It's actually quite easy for small organisations to offer flexible rewards packages too. Here's how to do it:

- ask your team for comments and ideas;

- cost those ideas, plus others you feel might be valued or welcomed;

- make sure you are providing everything the law says you should;

- take professional advice if you're worried or not sure about any aspect;

- negotiate individual rewards packages with your team.

VIRGIN

Several years ago one of the Virgin companies took over a building that used to be occupied by part of the Civil Service. It is a modern open-plan building with lots of architectural glass and steel. Despite that it was not an inspiring place with grey walls, blue carpets and paper everywhere.

Virgin changed all that. Bright paintwork, large murals, a staff cafeteria and informal meeting areas transfomed what had for years been a dull workplace into somewhere that people wanted to be. How can you make your workplace somewhere people want to go?

Individuality

The key to motivating people is to create and sustain a culture where they feel valued, recognised and properly rewarded. You must also give people the oppor-tunity to retain their individuality in the workplace. Take the trouble to discover and understand how race, faith and other personal factors need to be accommodated.

10 training opportunities you might overlook

Training and personal development can make a tremendous difference to the way people perform in their jobs. Don't forget that this also applies to you as the boss. However, if you thought that training had to involve spending lots of money, think again. Here are ten low cost options.

1. **Share** – if you're a small business, club together with others to organise training sessions. It will cost less and be more convenient that buying places on open courses.

2. **Ask suppliers** – they gain if you become more proficient. See if they have spare places on in-house training programmes that your people can attend.

3. **Teach each other** – the best training happens in the workplace with your own experts helping others catch up. Because this can happen spontaneously it's often overlooked.

4. **Work experience** – supervising students who visit you to gain work experience will develop the supervisory skills of those who do not usually manage people.

5. **School governor** – becoming a school governor provides excellent free management training. It makes people more objective in their own work.

6. **Charity trustee** – becoming a trustee enables people to develop their particular skill (for example finance, human relations or marketing) in a different context.

7. **Non-exec director** – if you work in the voluntary sector, why not become a non-executive director of a 'for profit' enterprise? Bring social awareness and learn about profitability.

8. **Grants** – there are many organisations able to give you training grants or provide free training. Look at local economic development websites.

9. **Read books** – some people find it easy to learn from books. Set up a company library – include training software and reward people who take items home to develop their skills.

10. **Online** – the internet is packed with learning opportunities. There are online training courses and web seminars you can attend virtually, and more.

To work out your organisation's training needs it's important to compare the skills you have with those your mission requires. Different organisations have different needs.

To map out the skills in your team you need to build a simple matrix with 'skills' on one axis and your team members on the other. Compare this with your operational needs and you begin to see where there are gaps. Aim not to be reliant on any one person for a particular skill.

	Word	Excel	Sales	French	German	Spanish
Judith	✓	✓		✓		
Michael	✓		✓			✓
Tom	✓	✓				
Ruth			✓	✓	✓	✓

It is also useful to assess the level of ability in each area. This enables you to encourage the experts to spend time developing the abilities of those less skilled.

Try to also identify skills within your team that are not currently needed by the organisation. They may become useful in the future.

10 common people-problems and how to solve them

Employing people can be one of the most rewarding things you do – it can also be very frustrating. People, unlike machines, do not always behave consistently. There are many problems you can encounter as a boss. Here are some tips for dealing with ten common ones.

1. **Poor performance** – before complaining, take time to find out how your employee views their performance. Have they a problem outside work? Do they need training?

2. **Poor timekeeping** – childcare, public transport and your body clock can all impact on timekeeping. Many organisations offer flexible working – could you?

3. **Wrong person** – we all make mistakes and hire the wrong person. Accept that this is probably as much your fault as theirs – take professional advice and sort it out quickly.

4. **Poor health** – as long as someone is not shirking, you need to be sympathetic. Consider sickness insurance which can replace the pay of someone who is long-term sick.

5. **Neurotic** – one in four people in the UK suffer from mental illness at some point. If you're on the receiving end of this recognise that, with professional help, many people come out of it better than before.

6. **Romance** – many people marry someone they meet at work. Office romances are part of life. Be ready with the tissues if it all goes wrong.

7. **Private calls** – don't get hung up if your people use your phone to sort out their private lives, unless it becomes excessive. Set ground rules to show what you consider to be reasonable.

8. **Theft** – any criminal activity should be dealt with quickly. Take advice – cover-ups and quick departures do not set a good example to others. Accept that you may be the last to know that something is going on.

9. **Tragedy** – people die, become disabled, divorce; they get mugged, robbed, raped and tragically attacked. Your role as employer is to listen and support. Help people when they're down and they'll help you more when they're up again.

10. **On reflection** – many people-problems are symptoms of poor management. Before roaming round the workplace lopping off heads, look in the mirror and make sure you're not the problem!

Other things that can go wrong and what to do

- **Accidents at work** – if someone is injured at work you could face a heavy fine if faulty equipment or poor workplace practice was the cause. When accidents happen, sort out the emergency and then investigate fully. Be sure to inform your insurer. Cooperate with outside agencies that get involved. Be prepared to face the media.

- **Accidents somewhere else** – yes, it can be worse. Road accidents involving your vehicles, industrial accidents that pollute rivers, fires and floods all are largely avoidable but do happen. Make sure you're fully insured and have a plan to fall back on.

- **Weather/war/etc.** – sometimes things happen that you cannot possibly predict or be prepared for. If the world looks like it's dealing you a rough hand, try to remain pragmatic and positive. Life's just like that sometimes.

Ways to be prepared

- **Insurance** – the more remote the risk, the lower the premium and the more devastating it can be if it happens. Get insured.

- **First aiders** – make sure you have qualified first aiders in your team. Also make sure that vehicles and workplaces have first aid kits and fire extinguishers.

- **Fire drills** – practice evacuating the building regularly. Avoid this when it's raining!

- **Security** – invest in good security alarms, lights, etc. Have them maintained regularly.

15 Surprises

predict and overcome those
unexpected hurdles

10 surprises employees spring and how to overcome them

It's true to say that taking on your first employee is one of the most demanding steps you have to take as you grow a business. Employees enable you to scale up your business to a point where, ultimately, it won't need you at all. Then you have the option to sell it.

If you're hesitant about employing people, or already do and are worried about what could go wrong, here are ten common surprises and how to avoid them.

1. **Coming in late every day** – what's changed at home to make mornings difficult? Partying every night? Find out and offer to help.

2. **Private phone calls** – remember the importance of 'give and take'. Is enough extra being done to justify latitude? If so, say nothing.

3. **Pilfering** – always make it clear what you consider to be reasonable in this respect. This is more of an issue in a sweet shop than a steelworks. Don't make rules and then break them yourself.

4. **Fraud** – if someone's robbing you or your business call the police. Never compromise.

5. **BO** – it sounds trivial but a worker with a personal hygiene problem is one of the stickiest issues most bosses have to face. Encourage workforce peers to hint or help.

6. **Moonlighting** – some specialists, for example graphic designers, take it as read that they can work for you in the day and themselves in the evening. Make your policy clear when you hire people. Avoid misunderstanding.

7. **Overfamiliarity** – as your business grows so too must the distance between you and your staff. There will simply be more things you cannot share. Manage the gap.

8. **Sickies** – it's always useful to record sick leave and check for patterns. Is it on the increase? Remember that workplace stress is a major cause of sick leave.

9. **Different values** – we all have to be tolerant of the views of employees. But when every last yoghurt carton has to be recycled and skimmed organic milk is all they will put in their fair trade coffee, your tolerance might be challenged. Negotiate a fair compromise.

10. **Faith** – we live in a multicultural society and some people will decide not to undertake certain duties for religious reasons. Respect faith requirements and adapt accordingly.

Employment tribunals await those accused of discriminating against their employees. The fact is that when things go 'legal' everyone loses out. Negative publicity, workplace tension and the hassle and frustration of the process can all cause lasting damage to your business.

The art of avoiding workplace conflict is to prevent it ever happening. You can do this by:

- taking up references before you hire someone, however convinced you are;

- encouraging them to tell you about their values at interview;

- trusting your instincts;

- setting out the ground rules in detail in a concise employee handbook;

- having professionally written contracts of employment.

If your business operates in a particularly sensitive area, for example medical research or meat production, you need to make doubly sure that you have every angle covered before you hire staff. It is not unknown for journalists to pose as workers and then expose what they present as bad practices.

JOHN

A successful motor dealer, John's daughter started going out with one of the mechanics in his workshop. This meant that family Sundays now often included a member of his workforce, who tactlessly discussed John's home arrangements on Monday mornings.

John felt trapped and uncomfortable. His daughter would, he reflected, look back on this relationship as an act of defiance. He wishes now he'd never given her a Saturday job on the service reception desk.

10 surprises customers spring and how to overcome them

It's important to make sure that your customers know the rules by which you trade with them. Of course rules are there to be bent. Here are ten ways your customers might try it on.

1. **Lost deliveries** – always get deliveries signed for and paperwork back from the carrier. It stops your customers' staff pinching goods and saying they never arrived.

2. **Rampant returns** – if a customer starts returning goods as 'faulty' it might be that they're not using them properly. Make time to visit and investigate.

3. **Cash crisis** – you deliver weekly and suddenly the customer is unable to pay. Do you keep supplying and hope they get back on track or pull out and cut your losses? Discuss!

4. **Legislation** – your customer points out that new legislation means you have to do something differently. Check that they're right, do it and pass on the cost.

5. **Relationships** – your salesman has been sleeping with their buyer and her husband has just found out. You've probably lost a customer!

6. **Crime** – your fastest-growing competitor has been jailed for dangerous driving. Can you jump in and take the customers he can no longer service? Find opportunities.

7. **Complaints** – sometimes people complain because they're expecting too much. Provide specifications and application data sheets to define what you consider possible.

8. **Goodbye** – sometimes customers drop you for no good reason. Always ask why and act on their feedback if it's beneficial. Write to tell the customer what you've changed.

9. **Pay twice** – not every surprise is a nasty one. However, if they mistakenly pay twice do send one payment back to demonstrate your honesty.

10. **Offer cash** – sometimes a customer offers to pay in cash. If they do, bank it!

Consultants have to work harder than most to manage customer expectations. Here are some pitfalls that can trip up the hapless consultant.

- **You overpromised** – in the excitement of doing the deal, you agree to solve all their problems. It's not surprising they're unhappy that you've only solved three of them.

- **You did what they wanted, not what they needed done** – consultancy is an area where you always have to look beyond the symptoms and work on the cause.

- **No terms of reference** – define the parameters of the project so that both parties understand. Only then can you be sure that you have finished the task.

- **One size doesn't fit all** – you've been on a course and want to deliver the same solution to all. All that happens is you become blasé and clients feel ignored.

GREG runs a recycling project. It's a social enterprise that takes redundant computers from large organisations. After cleaning and erasing data, they are sold on to people who otherwise could not afford to buy a computer. Migrant workers wishing to e-mail and Skype back home are his main market.

His local council, who give him dozens of computers a month, recruited a new head of information. He was more aware of computer security and insisted that Greg invested in additional software to erase data more reliably.

Greg asked another part of the same council to buy the software, a department responsible for migrant worker welfare. Otherwise he couldn't continue. They saw the benefit and paid for the software upgrade.

10 surprises suppliers spring and how to overcome them

Your suppliers may regard you as their best customer, but they may still let you down. Here are ten common surprises that suppliers can deliver to spoil your day.

1. **Lost deliveries** – goods really do go astray in transit and they cannot be replaced. Make sure you keep a buffer stock of all vital components.

2. **Quality drops** – if quality drops, work with your suppliers to resolve the problem. Visit them and see what is going wrong. Don't simply rant or change suppliers.

3. **Corporate deafness** – you've told them five times that something's wrong and they still keep doing it. Might mean it's time to find an alternative – you're no longer valued.

4. **Holiday** – make sure you know when suppliers are going on holiday and make sure you've got the gap covered. Many firms (for example printers) shut down for holidays.

5. **Price rises** – it's funny how prices always rise and never fall. Ask for a reason why.

6. **Service stops** – if you stick with products that become outdated be aware that, unless you buy enough, your supplier might find it uneconomic to continue supplying you.

7. **Over-engineering** – any product or service can be over-engineered. New features are added and the price goes up. See if products can also be simplified and made cheaper.

8. **Legislation** – as with customers, the rules concerning suppliers can change and scupper what you've enjoyed for years. Watch the horizon for new regulations.

9. **Going bust** – sometimes suppliers go bust. Make sure you're not reliant on one supplier, and if the worst happens delay paying the last bill. Liquidators will often not pursue an insolvent company's creditors.

10. **Soured friendship** – be cautious of enjoying too much of your supplier's hospitality. Sometimes the friendship that develops compromises objectivity at work.

Choosing suppliers for your business is not as easy as you might think. Try to:

- buy on quality, innovation and service as well as price;
- credit-check suppliers to make sure they're secure;
- take references from satisfied customers;
- let them make a profit too;
- write down the agreed 'service level agreement' so everyone understands.

Service level agreements sound grand but, in fact, are no more than documents that define:

- each aspect of the working relationship;
- what both parties have agreed to do;
- the penalties for failing to deliver;
- how the relationship will develop;
- how success is reviewed and improvement sought.

BARRY

Although now retired, Barry tells a wonderful, if sobering, story from when he was site manager running a major agrochemical manufacturing plant. Being the only chemical plant in the city, there were no similar businesses nearby so some specialist suppliers were difficult to find locally.

One particular firm handled all of Barry's 'high pressure' stainless steel repair work and the plant became dependent on their quick, local service. The firm encountered financial problems and Barry was faced with possibly losing a key supplier. He arranged for some of his management team to work with the supplier through the difficult patch. The supplier survived and the relationship is now even closer.

10 sleepless nights you can probably avoid

Surprises can come from many directions. Here are ten things that many never encounter, but if they come your way this checklist will help you deal with them.

1. **Jury service** – if summoned to join a jury, you are usually allowed to be excused once if you really cannot spare the time. Most people never get called.

2. **Crime** – as long as you have a security system and are sensible then your business is unlikely to be attacked. Keep data back-ups off site though, just in case.

3. **Poor health** – even the most severe flu epidemic is unlikely to affect everyone in your organisation at the same time. Experts suggest that at worst four out of five remain OK.

4. **Hacking** – apart from credit card fraud you are unlikely to be of interest to hackers. They tend to target big organisations. Do have a firewall and do be cautious.

5. **Divorce** – remembering that divorce can cost you half your company and make domestic life far from comfortable, it makes sense to dedicate time and effort to keeping your relationship on an even keel.

6. **War** – all out war is highly unlikely, although you do need to recognise that reservists are being called up for tours of duty in places where Britain is fighting.

7. **Terrorism** – does your business operate in sensitive locations? If not don't worry. If yes then take advice. You're probably more at risk on public transport than at work.

8. **Bankruptcy** – you will probably find enough work for next month and there are umpteen stages of decline before financial apocalypse. Don't panic!

9. **Strikes** – even if your workers are ardent members of a trade union, industrial action is unlikely to disrupt your business if you are fair, open and honest.

10. **Death** – some people worry about dying and what would happen to the business. Relax, in this eventuality it's someone else's problem!

Fear, reality and risk

In our dark moments, when tired, stressed and anxious, the world seems far more likely to deliver your enterprise a deadly blow than when you're on a roll. Remember these things.

- Reality is:
    - where you are right now;
    - your replay of what usually happens to others;
    - a world where there is time to plan, think and react.

- Fear is:
    - irrational;
    - brought on by unlikely events you might face;
    - delivered most often to those that invite it.

- Risk is:
    - measurable;
    - insurable;
    - manageable.

Focusing on risk is sensible when you are planning, but damaging if you think about it all the time. Remember the 80:20 rule – spend most of your time on the 20% of your activities/customers/products that carry 80% of your opportunity.

HENRY is a potter with his own gallery. In the past five years he has managed to:

- dry himself out with the help of Alcoholics Anonymous;
- get divorced;
- see a good friend die young;
- see his savings dwindle to zero.

Despite all these knocks he remains bullish and confident about his business's future. He knows that life can be tough, but equally he knows that bad is never too bad when you're actually there. If Henry can manage, so can you.

16 Helpers

people who might help you and how to encourage them

10 people eager to help you succeed

Many people are only too willing to offer you advice. Some will be more useful than others but all should be encouraged. Here are ten different people who will be eager to see you succeed and advice on how to manage their expectations.

1. **Parents** – they know you really well but may not be so familiar with entrepreneurship. Encourage them to focus on your well-being more than your bottom line.

2. **Bank manager** – clearly the bank's own interests will be top of your banker's agenda. Ask to share tips gleaned from the experiences of other customers.

3. **Accountant** – we all know that accountants tend to be cautious rather than daring. Accountants are best at helping you manage your costs, not increasing your sales.

4. **Financial advisers** – independent and trusted, friendly financial advisers can occupy a useful position. They are less biased than a bank and more entrepreneurial than most accountants. Good people to talk to when you need to raise cash.

5. **Consultants** – always judge a consultant by his or her track record. Experience and testimonials are more important than qualifications. Be wary of those who claim to be able to save you money – they will cost you money first!

6. **Friends** – rather like parents, friends know you better than your business. Encourage them to use their networks to introduce you to new customers.

7. **Customers** – always listen to your customers. Their feedback can be invaluable as you strive to develop your business. Invite constructive criticism and act on it.

8. **Suppliers** – make sure that your suppliers know you are receptive to advice. They'll be quick to share tips and good practice if they can see the benefit of your increased efficiency.

9. **Support agencies** – there's a whole world of Government-funded business advice out there. Much of it is good and almost all of it is independent and sincere.

10. **Yourself** – yes, you are probably your own best-qualified business adviser. Listen to your intuition and take time to reflect on what your experience tells you.

Choosing a business adviser

Whoever you choose to share your challenges with, make sure they have all or some of the following characteristics.

- **Empathy** – they are on your wavelength as a human being.
- **Knowledge** – of your business sector and of organisations your size.
- **Interest** – in your challenge, and not just because they might profit from it.
- **Enthusiasm** – and a willingness to explore new ideas with you rather than recycle old ones.
- **Contacts** – with other people able to help you make it happen.
- **Open mind** – so they will buy your motives and not impose their own.
- **Track record** – successful as agents of change with evidence that they can share.
- **Ethics** – so you won't be led to places you find uncomfortable
- **Wealth** – the best advisers are those that don't need your project to pay the bills.
- **Radar** – the ability to see what's just over your business horizon.

When preparing a brief for your adviser, remember to include:

- an overview of what your business does;
- your vision for the future;
- the key issues you feel you are facing;
- how you feel an adviser can help;
- your budget and what you expect to see from your investment.

MARTIN

Nearing retirement age, Martin has enjoyed a long and successful senior management career. No longer working full-time, he now enjoys helping others to succeed in business as well as he has over the years. Comfortably off, the fees he charges reflect more the ability of his client to pay than his desire to dramatically boost his income.

Martin works with those he finds interesting and where he knows his experience and skill will add the most value. He has a great network and acts as a 'general practitioner' for his clients, introducing others as the need arises.

There are many people like Martin out there. All you have to do is find him or her.

10 things consultants do well

However hard you try, it's really difficult to remain objective when you are so close to the coalface. A good consultant can help you see and deal with the blockages every business has. Here are ten examples.

1. **Marketing** – communicating your strengths to prospective customers requires specialist expertise. Few entrepreneurs fail to benefit from help in this area.

2. **Innovation** – doing old things in new ways, or simply doing new things, requires you to stop long enough to think. Consultants give you the time, and they have been there before.

3. **Cost control** – a fresh pair of eyes can often see clearly where profits are leaking from your company.

4. **Funding** – finding the money to grow needs a combination of accountancy skills and a good knowledge of the funding playing field. What's more, lenders may actually have more confidence in the consultant than you!

5. **Recruitment** – choosing the right people is often better done by others. After all, recruitment consultants do it all the time.

6. **Training** – reconciling your business needs with the skills available, and planning how to plug the gaps, is crucial. Why not get an expert to help?

7. **Firing** – it may seem a cop-out but if you've got a problem member of staff then a specialist in employment law can help to sort it out.

8. **IT** – technology is constantly changing. Make sure someone is keeping you up to date.

9. **Property** – whether buying, selling, building, altering or adapting most people get outside help with sorting out property issues.

10. **Introductions** – the best consultants are able to introduce you to people who they feel can collaborate with you in some way. Consultants can broker project partnerships.

Consultants are like cars – they come in all shapes and sizes and there's usually a choice within your price range. As with cars, it's no good buying a cheap one if you want to make a long journey. Equally, the top-of-the-range model might be good for your ego, but if you simply want to potter around the block it's a bit of a waste. Here are some places you might look to find a consultant.

- **Ask a friend** – to recommend someone they've been happy with.

- **Support agencies** – have lists of vetted consultants who they know can do the job.

- **Accountants** – usually know who can deliver and who to avoid.

- **Networks** – generate many useful contacts.

- **Professional bodies** – often have experts in the field you are exploring.

Consultants tend to come in two types – strategists and tacticians. Here's how to choose between them.

Strategists	Tacticians
Help you decide where to go	Grab your hand and take you there
Write impressive reports	Write impressive operational plans
Are often academically gifted	Often have battle scars
Can rarely help you to deliver their plan	Can implement but not write the plan

10 things to share because you don't need to buy

We all buy things we hardly use. Think how much more profitable your business could be if you shared stuff instead? Here are ten things you could share.

1. **Machines** – why not club together with neighbours and share that forklift truck? Sharing means you can afford bigger, better and sooner!

2. **People** – why not pool labour with others? It's unlikely you'll all be busy at once.

3. **Postal collection** – share a franking machine and have the postman pick up your mail from one convenient point. Share the cost, enjoy the convenience.

4. **Learning** – put together your own groups for training programmes. Have them delivered where and when it suits you. This will be more convenient and probably save money.

5. **Suppliers** – buy together in bulk for bigger discounts.

6. **Customers** – why not team up with others who sell to the same audience and stage an event. You all invite your own customers and can sell to each other's.

7. **Intelligence** – keep the jungle drums beating on your business park. Don't keep hot intelligence to yourself – share it out.

8. **Canteen** – everyone has to eat but at work most people make do with eating sandwiches at their desk. Create a shared canteen with other firms and network as you nosh.

9. **Security** – neighbourhood watch schemes in business areas can reduce insurance costs and prevent crime. Ask the police for information.

10. **Waste** – is someone else's waste product your raw material? Help them and yourself.

Cross sectors

Don't just collaborate with people who have a similar organisation to your own. There are huge benefits to be gained from businesses, social enterprises and charities working together. For example, you can help each other by:

● sharing resources that are common to all;

● link fund-raising to product promotion to widen the appeal;

- establishing unique joint ventures and projects;

- mentoring each other and benefiting from a fresh perspective on your work;

- using work experience to give each other's staff insights into new worlds.

LINDA

For ten years Linda has managed a machinery ring in Caithness. More than 130 farmers pay an annual membership fee and ring Linda when they need help on the farm. 'Most are one-man bands,' Linda said, 'so sometimes they need manpower as well as machines. I ring round and find what they need from someone who has the time or equipment. The machinery ring takes a commission for arranging each job.'

If the machinery ring did not exist these farmers would each need to buy their own machinery. By offering labour as well, farmers' sons, who might otherwise have had to leave the land, can work at home and for neighbours.

Machinery rings are common in farming communities. Could your business community do something similar?

10 things to look for when finding a mentor

Many of the most successful people in the world have a mentor. There is a lot of confusing jargon around mentoring and coaching. What you really need is someone who has the following qualities.

1. **Focuses on you** – because your work and home life are inevitably interlinked.

2. **Is objective** – and will encourage you wherever you choose to go.

3. **Tells you the tough stuff** – sometimes there are things you need to know that others are reluctant to say. A good mentor will make positive suggestions about things you might change.

4. **Lasts** – as long as you need them. Good mentoring relationships can last for years. Can your mentor work with you for as long as you need them?

5. **Is willing to be outgrown** – it's also true to say that you will in time outgrow your mentor. Both need to see this as success and then move on.

6. **Is older than you** – someone older than you probably has more experience. They also want different things from work and life and so are in no way competing with you.

7. **Says no** – if you're the boss you may not have many people close to you willing to say no. Sometimes it's good to be challenged in this way.

8. **Has trodden the same path** – if you work in a particular field, someone who is experienced and better established, perhaps retired, might be able to help you along the same path.

9. **Shows commitment** – perhaps not strictly what mentors are for, but sometimes it's actually better if they handle the tricky situation for you. Watch, learn and do it yourself next time.

10. **Likes you** – your mentor needs to like you, otherwise it simply won't work.

The process of finding a mentor can be arduous. We all tend to aim too low and assume that the people we admire the most will refuse. Remember that you can have several mentors, each helping you cope with a different aspect of your life. Here are some ways to find one.

- **Become a fan** – if there's someone you really admire, make sure you tell them. Get to know them and ask if they could help you to follow their example. Many successful people will give a little of their time to help others. Don't assume they'll say no.

- **Be analytical** – write down a list of the things you feel that you need help with. Then research people in your area likely to be good at them.

- **Network** – most mentors are introduced by someone who knows both of you. The wider your network, the greater the chance of a successful introduction.

- **Get a life coach to pitch** – asking someone who has set out to be a coach to sell themselves to you will reveal areas for action you many not have considered. Pay them for the hour, but only go further if it really feels right.

- **Ask around** – bank managers, accountants and consultants often know people who might make good mentors. Many of these people are recently retired, but not ready to stop work.

JENNY

After a career as a senior HR director, Jenny took early retirement. She built a portfolio of organisations for whom she undertakes project work. In the course of these she sometimes meets people she feels able to help with their self-development.

Often a mentoring relationship grows out of contact with those she has identified who could benefit from her mentoring support. She agrees a programme of regular meetings and e-mail support and charges them a monthly fee. She agrees goals and timescale at the start.

17 Balance

when to work and when to play

10 signs that you are getting stressed and how to cope

Running any kind of organisation can be pretty unforgiving. It's not surprising that stress is a common, although rarely talked about, problem. The truth is that as you grow your enterprise you also grow yourself – that's one reason it can become stressful. Here are ten common signs of stress and how to cope with them.

1. **Frequent headaches** – if you are reaching for the aspirin, almost without thinking, it might mean you're doing too much. Get some fresh air and reflect on your day.

2. **Butterflies** – are important if you are to perform well in important meetings, but if you're stressed you can feel them far more often. Try to keep work in perspective.

3. **Self-medicating** – increasing consumption of coffee, alcohol, nicotine and even sugar can be signs of stress. Be aware of your consumption and what it might be telling you.

4. **Overreacting** – you fly off the handle when really the issue is not that important. Switching off seems difficult and everything's coming at you too quickly.

5. **Paranoia** – you are beginning to feel oppressed. Is the world really plotting your downfall? Or are you imagining the worst? Step back and try to become objective.

6. **In bed** – you might notice that two things are more difficult to manage. One is sleep and the other mostly affects men only! Both are classic symptoms of stress.

7. **Digestive problems** – from indigestion to irritable bowel, your guts act as a barometer of your mood. Stress can cause digestive problems. Treat the cause and the symptoms.

8. **Poor judgement** – if you are stressed then your ability to make decisions is hampered. The consequences can be stressful in themselves. Try to defer big decisions or involve others.

9. **Escapism** – when severely stressed facing work can be difficult. If you feel the urge to take time off, or even run away, seek professional help.

10. **Feedback** – if you work with others they'll notice you becoming more stressed. They'll probably also be astute enough to identify the cause. Be brave and ask them.

Many of the physical symptoms of stress occur in response to the production of adrenaline, perhaps compounded by your intake of caffeine, tobacco and alcohol. While we all have panic attacks from time to time (and that's a normal part of business life) stress is something different. Stress levels can rise gradually so that you hardly notice the change. The result is that your effectiveness falls and you become less user-friendly. Both make it harder to achieve the goals you set yourself.

There are countless books, websites and other sources of advice dealing with stress. To get you started, here are a few tips that can help you avoid getting unduly stressed.

- **Realism** – set out to perform well but do not be overambitious or set unrealistic goals.

- **Prioritise** – do today what has to be done today. Delegate as much as you are able and don't fret about tomorrow's task today.

- **Exercise** – however busy you are, make time for regular physical exercise in your working week. Exercising also provides good thinking time.

- **Share** – we all need a confidant, someone you know you can discuss things with openly who will be supportive and help you see things as they really are. Get a mentor.

- **Measure** – measure out the business journey and highlight the milestones. Measure progress all the time so you can see what you've achieved, as well as what's pressing.

Getting help

If stress is your problem then seek help. A search of the internet or local telephone directory will point you towards:

- charities that provide counselling and support for stress and mental illness;

- professionals who, for a fee, will help you unpick and resolve the issue;

- gyms where you can work out your stress and take time out.

Unresolved stress can damage your health, both physically and mentally. Don't let it!

10 ways to enjoy your work

We've all read about the importance of achieving a good work–life balance. However, in reality the pressures of a growing organisation can make it difficult for everyone in it, not just those at the top. Here are ten ways to make sure everyone enjoys their work.

1. **Be comfortable** – you spend a lot of time at work so why not create a comfortable environment? This is particularly important if you spend a lot of time at a desk.

2. **Be confident** – take a pride in what your organisation does and be sure that your efforts are for a worthwhile cause. You won't be happy unless you are confident in your mission.

3. **Be sociable** – however busy you are, spare time to talk to others. Networking keeps your life in perspective. It also allows you to bump into new opportunities.

4. **Be ethical** – you have to live with yourself. Don't deviate from your personal values.

5. **Be helpful** – try to surprise one person each day by doing something unexpectedly helpful. This could be a colleague, a customer or supplier. Build respect.

6. **Be healthy** – consider private medical insurance so you can get those niggling health problems sorted out quickly. Don't let bad health pull you down.

7. **Be adventurous** – try new things, although not too many at once! Don't get stuck in a rut where work becomes tedious and you find yourself yearning for the weekend.

8. **Be mobile** – you can change the scenery by moving your office or workshop round from time to time. This avoids the build-up of clutter and also stops you getting bored with the view.

9. **Be green-fingered** – don't just put flowers in the office, make a garden outside if there's room. Could you hold meetings outside on nice days? Everyone would enjoy that!

10. **Be there** – sometimes things can seem too much and even the strongest willed of us feel like staying in bed. You can only improve work if you're where the action is. Be there!

We are all conditioned to think that work is work and that life is something different. For true entrepreneurs there is no distinction between the two. That is not to say they work all the time – more that they probably enjoy each of the week's activities equally. Established, successful entrepreneurs:

- love everything they do;
- forget what makes money and what does not;
- often work at weekends and are just as likely to play during the week;
- see opportunities in everything they see or do;
- dress confidently knowing that no one can impose rules.

You will know that you are successful and have arrived when:

- money becomes a want, not a need;
- you'd like to be recognised as a success;
- giving help to others makes you as happy as helping yourself;
- people want to network with you and not the other way around;
- banks give you back the loan guarantees you made earlier.

RICHARD

Now in his late fifties, Richard has worked hard to build up his business. To his delight, his son Will asked a few years ago if he could leave his job and come home to help run the firm. Will soon made his mark and proved he could handle the business day to day, freeing up Richard's time to explore new business opportunities.

Richard has become active in several local business networks and industry training initiatives. He really enjoys helping Will and others go through the stages of business growth he experienced when younger. To his surprise, this willingness to give has raised his profile locally and led to his company winning new clients. Richard is a very content entrepreneur.

10 holiday ideas for when you can't afford to take time off

Experts tell us that several short breaks can be as refreshing as three weeks on the beach. Here's ten ways to squeeze holiday time into your busy schedule.

1. **Long weekends** – leave the office at 3 pm on Friday and go somewhere exciting for a couple of nights. Monday will be really productive if you've been away for the weekend.

2. **Take some customers** – why not take a group of customers to visit an overseas supplier? The supplier will probably pay part of the cost and the customers may order more!

3. **Extra days** – if you're travelling on business, take an extra day to see the sights. Take your partner with you to reconnoitre while you are working.

4. **An hour's enough** – if you have a day out and about, make sure there's a free hour at some point in the day. Enjoy a walk, go shopping or eat ice cream in the park.

5. **Join the army** – the various volunteer reserve forces can give you excellent free training in your spare time, and trips to new places too. Learn, earn and play all at the same time.

6. **Cook a meal** – even if you cannot spare any time off, you can take the time to read a recipe book in the morning, shop in the afternoon and prepare your partner a surprise meal in the evening. Over dinner talk about holidays!

7. **Entertain** – while no one does the blow-out corporate lunches experienced (or endured!) by many in the 1980s, a convivial evening with a customer at the theatre or a football match allows you to combine work with time off.

8. **Think technology** – if you really cannot bear to be out of touch then move your office to your holiday destination. Call forwarding and internet access mean you can sit by the pool and work as if at your desk.

9. **Pretend you're sick** – imagine you've broken your leg. Organise cover at work and take a holiday. Do not break your leg.

10. **Take a walk** – a lunchtime walk to the travel agent's office is one short break that might lead to another!

Holidays are actually great business opportunities. You should not need an excuse to take time out to enjoy yourself. Here are more reasons why holidays are important.

- **Inspiration** – see how you can take ideas from other areas back to your business.

- **Networking** – get to know other holidaymakers. Are they potential clients?

- **Blue sky** – clear your mind, watch the clouds and imagine.

- **Seek novelty** – regulations vary across the globe. See how others do what you do.

- **Challenge your thinking** – experience the extreme and put your worklife in perspective.

IAN worked in the food industry so took a great interest in what he saw in American supermarkets while on holiday. He saw a healthy snack product sold for children's lunchboxes that seemed very popular.

After detailed research, he started a business in England making similar products and has watched his business grow. If he hadn't gone on holiday he would have missed the opportunity.

18 Social responsibility

how to help yourself by helping others

10 ways to build your business by helping others

Read any large company annual report and it will talk about 'corporate social responsibility'. Read further and you'll discover how this means they've been 'doing good' for others, partly because it enhances their reputation.

Every organisation, however small, can benefit from being more socially responsible. Here are ten very practical ways to help yourself by helping others.

1. **Mentoring** – mentor someone managing a voluntary or community organisation. They may face very different challenges to you but you'll both learn from working together.

2. **Donating products** – if you make a consumer product, give away a redundant product to someone who would not normally be able to use it. Make sure you get news coverage.

3. **Sharing knowledge** – share your experience and advice with groups where other volunteers might be potential customers. For example, the Prince's Trust recruits business mentors for budding entrepreneurs from disadvantaged backgrounds.

4. **Offering work experience** – it's not just kids that need work experience. People rebuilding their confidence after mental ill health also need reintroducing to the world of work. Providing work experience shows that you care. People prefer to trade with people that care.

5. **Hosting visits** – allow others to see how you run your organisation. The visit will inevitably be promoted to a wide audience and many who come will be potential customers.

6. **Sharing scrap** – if you make things, your waste materials or packaging could be useful to a social enterprise that reuses materials. Reduce your costs and increase your profile.

7. **Teaching kids** – explaining what you do and why to a group of 13-year-olds is a great experience. It will certainly make you think because kids ask lots of questions and demand credible answers. It's good to have your basic assumptions challenged.

8. **Raising money** – if you employ people, get them to agree on a local good cause and help them to raise funds as a team. There are lots of things to do. It really builds a team.

9. **Putting a bench outside your shop** – make it possible for people to rest outside your shop. It makes it look busier and everyone will look in the window.

10. **Sponsorship** – funding the youth football team's shirts and printing your firm's name on the back is perhaps the most obvious way of trading support for publicity.

As soon as you recognise that your business forms part of a wider society, you begin to see that the opportunities are endless. The concept of helping to raise your organisation's profile through helping others is perhaps a little more complex than many of the topics in this book. It is, however, not to be overlooked. To illustrate the point here are some specific examples of things that have been done before.

Activity	Benefit to the business
A baker gives leftover cakes to a hostel for rough sleepers	Everyone knows that the cakes they buy in the morning really are freshly baked
Accountant runs free advice sessions for start-up businesses	This is the first accountant the new entrepreneur meets – they get to meet lots of potential new clients
An ad agency does all the marketing for a city charity appeal for nothing	The campaign is widely seen and wins an award – the agency wins work from bigger charities with budgets to invest
An engineering works allows a local college to train students in its workshops after hours	The firm can look for potential employees and all become familiar with their workplace
An IT company helps in a school	Parents hear about this and may buy from them

10 ways to entertain your customers for free

Creating social opportunities to bond with those who we want to do business with can be difficult. Many prefer not to accept corporate gifts and the days of lavish lunches are long past. Here are ten politically correct and free ways to entertain customers.

1. **Fund-raising dinner** – people will buy tickets for a dinner if some of the money goes to a good cause. People will also be more likely to attend!

2. **Join a club** – even if you are not into 'gentleman's clubs' you can join something that provides appropriate hospitality opportunities. For example, friends of art galleries can often take guests to exhibitions for free.

3. **Ask them to pay!** – if they recognise that you have pared your costs to the bone and have made only a modest profit, then why shouldn't they buy lunch for you?

4. **Supplier seminar** – get your suppliers to organise seminars for your customers. Make sure they include food and drink, and time to network and socialise.

5. **Trade body events** – take your customers to hear industry pundits speak at trade events.

6. **Recognise achievement** – give an award for excellence in your field. Invite others to the presentation. Have the buffet sponsored by your bank.

7. **Take them on a walk** – perhaps not viewed by all as entertaining but why not encourage your customers to join you in a sponsored walk? Get tired together!

8. **Hijack a trade seminar** – organise your own 'fringe' programme around an event you and your customers are attending. It's cheaper than doing it on your own.

9. **Travel together** – people seem reluctant to share cars yet offering a lift to those you want to influence, when you are both going to a trade show for example, converts travelling time into selling time.

10. **Give kittens** – if your cat surprises you by having kittens then invite your business contacts to provide good homes for them. You'll always then have a good reason to phone.

Fund-raising events can create fantastic opportunities to bring together customers, prospects, suppliers and others important to your success. As suggested in the checklist, those you invite will buy their ticket and pay their way. They might also provide raffle and tombola prizes. These events take a lot of organising and the benefiting good cause should be able to help. Here are some other benefits of fund-raising events:

- big name speakers will often waive their fee if they approve of the cause;

- people will come to network with each other – they will talk positively about you;

- guests of guests are often people you've never met;

- you get plenty of profile and get to speak to everyone;

- the presentation of the cheque may be featured in your local or trade press;

- following-up to ask if people enjoyed themselves can lead to talking business;

- others may sponsor certain elements of the event so you can raise more money;

- sharing the event with a non-competitor lets you influence each other's networks;

- invitations can carry subtle advertising;

- everyone thinks you're a generous person – this makes business easier to do.

LEN

A haulier with a fleet of tipper trucks and hire skips, Len does not have a sophisticated business, nor is it particularly important to any of his customers. Few would choose to socialise with him.

Recognising this, he organised a charity barbecue in his yard with food, music and a guest celebrity. He planned to raise money for the local hospice. He invited everyone he had ever dealt with, offering tickets at £20 per head.

Some 200 people bought tickets and most turned up. His costs were £10 per head so he was able to present the hospice with a cheque for £2,000. Parked around the outside of his yard was his fleet of trucks. People said they had not realised how large and modern his fleet was. On Monday morning he booked jobs for three new customers – each had been a guest at the barbecue. As Len mused, 'Why advertise when they will pay to come and see what I do?'

10 special things about social enterprises

Social enterprises are special. They are also a fast-growing business sector. There are many definitions, but in a nutshell, a successful social enterprise trades profitably for the benefit of many, not just the owners. Here are ten things that make social enterprises special.

1. **Passion** – they are usually started by people wishing to bring about lasting social change. Their passion and desire to do good gives the enterprise determination and strength.

2. **Access to funding** – set up a social enterprise and you can seek funding from some grant-making trusts as well as from the bank. You have more flexibility.

3. **Transparency** – if formally registered as a 'community interest company' with UK Companies House then you are committed to retaining profits rather than taking them all out.

4. **Customer appeal** – if you match the service offered by a global brand of, say, coffee shop then customers will prefer to drink coffee in your cafe if you're a social enterprise.

5. **More sustainable** – you have the flexibility to trade, pay directors and more. You can be more commercial than a charity and that makes your enterprise more sustainable.

6. **Bridge the gap** – a charity and 'for profit' business can set up a jointly owned social enterprise, pooling skills and sharing the return. It's a unique opportunity.

7. **More motivated staff** – in general, people choose to work for a social enterprise because they share the values. Everyone sees it as more than just a job.

8. **Less competition** – there are fewer social enterprises and they are different from 'for profit' businesses. Because you are 'different', you encounter less market competition.

9. **You can reward yourself** – charity rules can make it difficult to reward yourself. Set up a social enterprise and the rules allow you to pay salaries and dividends.

10. **Be green** – because you are not just about making money, it's easier to make sure that you follow good environmental practice. You can set a good example for others to follow.

By their very nature, social enterprises can be easier to set up than 'for profit' businesses. This is because they can attract 'pump priming' grants. Investors also take a longer-term view. Here are opportunities you may spot if you establish a social enterprise.

- **Venture philanthropists** – people who lend money to social enterprises on more favourable terms than if you were setting up a 'for profit' business.

- **Rent holidays** – public sector landlords in particular may give you a rent holiday to make it easier to establish your social enterprise.

- **Business support** – people already established may be inclined to give you practical support, discounted services and more.

- **Grants** – if you partner with a charity they may have access to capital grants that can fund your set-up costs. Unlike loans, grants don't have to be repaid.

- **Invitations to share resources** – neighbouring organisations may well offer to share stuff with you.

To succeed as a social entrepreneur you need to be able to clearly demonstrate that you are focused, businesslike and objective. If people view you as a woolly minded idealist, they will not give you their support.

CHARLIES is a growing chain of juice and smoothie bars. Owners Greg and Clare set up a jointly owned social enterprise with a mental health charity in a city where they had no outlets. The charity had a capital grant to establish a cafe where their clients, people recovering from mental ill health, could gain valuable work experience.

By working together, Charlies was able to open a new outlet without borrowing money and the charity gets the employment opportunities it was seeking. Both are able to bring their very different skills and strengths to the joint venture.

Being a social enterprise has also encouraged more customers to use the outlet. Everybody is a winner.

10 benefits of making a philanthropic gesture

Many of the world's most successful entrepreneurs have set up their own charitable foundations. This enables them to make a difference in the world by sharing their fortunes with those less fortunate. You're probably not a multi-millionaire but that doesn't mean you can't afford to be philanthropic. Here are ten good reasons to share your profits with others.

1. **Feel good** – using the proceeds of your success to help others makes you feel good.

2. **Lasting** – however well known you have become in your business sector, you will soon be forgotten when you sell, retire or die. Giving can make sure you are remembered.

3. **Tax** – you need to take advice but giving to charitable causes is incredibly tax efficient.

4. **Children** – of course you want to give your children a good start. But give them too much and you may spoil them. Have them help you choose the causes you support.

5. **How much is enough?** – when you've made sufficient to realise your life's dreams, the rest just becomes an investment portfolio you worry about. Let someone else invest it.

6. **World-changing** – governments can never make as big a difference as an individual. They don't have your focus, passion or drive. You can respond quickly to need.

7. **Direct action** – don't just lobby for a new playground for your local school. Build one!

8. **Vital** – some sectors, for example the arts, rely on patronage to survive.

9. **Recognition** – if this is important to you, most major gifts can be publicly acknowledged. Anonymity is preferred by some.

10. **Protection** – for things that might otherwise be lost for ever. It is a fact that increasingly it is only philanthropy that keeps many worthwhile projects running.

If you want to avoid the flood of begging letters that becoming philanthropic can prompt, consider giving money via a Community Foundation. Most places have one. You then simply give them the money and they invite groups to bid for grants. They are professional and can assess applications impartially. You remain part of that grant-making process.

Area	Low budget	Medium budget	Massive budget
Education	Buy books for local school	Sponsor a curriculum area	Build a school
	Provide an item of equipment	Equip a laboratory	Fund a university chair
Health	Provide a TV for the doctor's waiting room	Fund a specialist clinic	Build a hospice
	Provide an item of specialist equipment	Support work overseas	Build a medical mission
Arts	Pay for art therapy	Fund an arts worker	Build a gallery
	Sponsor an exhibition	Fund an 'artist in residence'	Fund a monument

CHRIS was invited to join other young entrepreneurs to build with them a 'young bloods' fund within their local Community Foundation. A group of 50 people, including Chris, each agreed to give £2,000 a year for five years. This will build a fund of half a million pounds which will be invested in an endowment. Future 'young bloods' will also be encouraged to join and give.

Chris did not set out to do business with other members of the group, but as he came to get to know them through foundation events he found that several became customers of his company. He doubts that investing the same money in marketing could have produced as good a return.

19 Exit

selling your successful business

10 ways to decide it's time to sell

Businesses have a natural lifespan. It's often best to sell up when they reach a point where dramatic change is needed to avoid decline. Here are ten signs that it's time to sell.

1. **You get an offer** – someone else has spotted the potential to add your enterprise to theirs. The value your enterprise adds to theirs might mean this is a generous offer.

2. **You're bored** – it happens. The business is no longer exciting and the problems seem to be greater than the opportunities. You need a change, and so too does your business.

3. **You're old** – why work longer than you really need? If your business is worth enough to fund a long and happy retirement why not cash in and develop new interests?

4. **Investment needed** – to stay competitive you need major investment and it would make more sense to become part of a larger organisation. You need to acquire or be acquired.

5. **Market maturing** – you've had the best years and now it's time to adapt or perish. Alternatively, sell while there's still some market left.

6. **Big players?** – you've started in a niche market and grown to the point that the big players are getting annoyed. Maybe they'd like to buy you out? Ask them.

7. **Opportunity knocks** – there's a great 'once in a lifetime' chance to get involved with something new. If you're sure it's not merely a case of 'grass looking greener' then sell to release time and cash.

8. **Eager beavers?** – your successor, who you've been grooming for years, is snapping at your heels. You may need to allow a management buyout now or risk losing the people.

9. **Pressure at home** – has your partner retired already? If so, it's not unreasonable for him or her to want you to do the same. Remember that good relationships are worth more than business success.

10. **You just want to** – if it feels right and you're sure it's what you want to do, and if you're the majority shareholder, then it's your prerogative to call the shots.

When people buy a small business, they often try to commit the owner to staying on to make sure that the value in the business is retained. In other words, that you stay around to keep the customers, staff and suppliers loyal. Owners rarely want to stay and so this can become a contentious point in the negotiations. The less the business depends on you, the less likely this is to happen.

There are a number of ways of buying a business. It's not often as straightforward as someone writing you a large cheque! Here are some examples.

- **Cash upfront** – you get paid and walk away. This is the ideal, but it rarely happens!

- **Earn out** – you are paid from future turnover. This often happens when professional practices are purchased. It links the price to client retention.

- **Shares** – you get paid in shares and end up owning part of the parent company. Unless it's stock market listed, those shares may be difficult to sell.

ANGUS

Having started a successful mail order retail business, Angus was flattered to be approached by a market leader. The company did not have a mail order division and recognised that buying one from Angus was preferable to building one from scratch.

The deal involved a lot of money but most of it was to be paid over the next few years and would depend on the division's performance. The deal also meant that Angus would have to stay on to run the business for a few years.

After much thought Angus turned the offer down. He didn't want to become an employee – nor did he want others to decide his payout based on the profitability of his business which would be part of a group largely beyond his control.

---

10 things that add value to your business

Business transfer agents and accountants apply all sorts of formulae to value a business. The reality is that for most people the price you get when you sell is the price that someone is prepared to pay. Here are ten business value boosters.

1. **Profits** – the ability to make good profits consistently is the most important factor in establishing a business's value.

2. **Potential** – the second most important factor is hard evidence that profits will continue to grow. What indicators are there that the future looks even better than the past?

3. **People** – if you've employed and motivated really good people and you hardly need to visit the office, your business is worth more than if you've been a control freak.

4. **Premises** – is your business operating from a location that's worth more than the business itself? If your cycle repair shop could be bulldozed to make way for a supermarket, get excited.

5. **Intellectual property** – any patents or trade marks need to be registered so that your buyer knows that those intangible assets are fully protected from imitation.

6. **Loyal customers** – customer inertia has a huge value. If much of your business is repeat business then a buyer can confidently expect those customers to remain loyal.

7. **Reputation** – if you've worked hard to maintain a high profile in your target market, you probably have a good reputation. Reputation does affect value.

8. **Market position** – if you command a price premium then your business is less susceptible to market downturn. Being in the top third of your sector is worth more than being bottom.

9. **Location** – some businesses are easy to relocate, others need to be where they are. Location is important, as is room to grow and a ready source of potential employees.

10. **Your motivation** – if you've lost the plot then your business will be worth less than if you're still out there fighting the business battle. It's best to quit while you're ahead!

Profits versus value

Hopefully, your business gives you a good income and a pleasing degree of control over how your spend your time. To be honest though, many can achieve this as an employee so why are you in business? The right answer is to create an enterprise that you can sell. This means that, at some point in the future, you can swap the overdraft for a pile of cash.

As you build your business you should never lose sight of the need to add value and create an enterprise (or enterprises) that can be sold one day. This should be the carrot at the end of your stick. There are some personal qualities you need to develop if you are to build real value into your business. These include:

- **objectivity** – you must let your head run your business, not your heart;

- **focus** – stick to what you do best and do it better, avoid distraction;

- **separation** – the business is your baby but you need to give it room to be independent of you – don't muddle up what's yours and what's the firm's.

> **MAURICE**
>
> A lifelong salesman, Maurice started a business at the age of 50 when he became fed up with working for others. His wife liked making soft toys and he started a business selling soft toy kits to independent haberdashers and chain stores.
>
> With an active social life and plenty of 'out of work' interests he kept the business simple renting a modern industrial unit and hiring agency staff to cut out and assemble kits. A short product range and very low overhead costs meant that he could match demand closely with labour and thus his business was very profitable. When he decided to retire, all he really had to sell was a market share. The business was quickly acquired at a good price by a larger firm with spare production capacity.

Top tip

People buy potential and performance, not your personal passion!

10 ways to find a buyer

Ideally you want to market your business discreetly, rather than hanging a 'for sale' sign on the door. Here are ten ways to sell without making it obvious.

1. **Ask the accountant** – some accountants specialise in matchmaking between sellers and buyers of small businesses. They recruit buyers through seminars and local knowledge, and then broker the deal.

2. **Chat to suppliers** – if you sit between your suppliers and the marketplace, they might be interested in buying you out. Start the chat with 'just suppose . . . '.

3. **Chat to big customers** – if you are a vital supplier to a customer it might appeal to them to diversify and take control of your firm. It could strengthen their position.

4. **Ask the team** – you will know your people well. Are they likely to be able to put together a management buyout? For many smaller firms this is the best way to sell.

5. **Box numbers** – you've seen the ads in the paper. They describe the business vaguely and give a box number for enquiries. It's cheap enough so try it!

6. **Rising stars** – who's the wunderkind in your sector? More importantly, who is backing them? Let it be known that you might be receptive to merger talks.

7. **Corporate** – if you've grown to a size where you are annoying a far larger competitor, they may well be willing to buy you out to regain market control.

8. **Agents** – as with houses and commercial property, there are agents who specialise in selling businesses. They are good at attracting potential buyers.

9. **Insolvency practitioner** – if things are not going well and you're really bailing out, an insolvency practitioner can often help you to plan a clean escape by selling your business.

10. **Network** – put yourself about and listen to what people say. Don't attend networking events to promote that you want to sell, more to see what intelligence you can glean.

Working out what your business is worth has already been covered. It is essentially all about its potential to deliver future returns to the new owner. Your business will be worth more to someone who wants:

- **to buy it** – for maybe purely emotional reasons;
- **to plug a gap** – in their regional, national or international network;
- **more control** – of the market or supply chain;
- **your people** – because they have valuable skills;
- **your customers** – because winning them 'in battle' might cost more.

Selling up is not a quick process. It usually takes several months from the time you find your buyer to the cheque arriving. The buyer will want to delve deeply into your business's affairs, usually accompanied by professional advisers. Make sure you have at least your accountant helping you through the process.

After you have sold your business you should never:

- dwell on the deal and question your decision;
- be envious if the business suddenly takes off;
- be smug if it consequently goes bust;
- compete with your former company;
- speak badly of the new team.

10 reasons to merge your business with another

One way to grow quickly, as well as to create your own exit route, is to merge your business with another. When merging always make sure you consider these ten points.

1. **You'll get on** – if you are going to stay with the merged business you need to be sure you'll get on with your new business partners.

2. **2 + 2 = 5** – there has to be a clear benefit, either in terms of additional skills or reduced overhead costs. If 2+ 2 = 4, don't do it.

3. **Bigger is better** – if you are a minnow among sharks then getting bigger quickly can protect you both from being gobbled up.

4. **The figures add up** – take professional advice from your accountant, who will also check out the deal and protect your interests. Accept that this will be frustrating!

5. **Compliance costs** – some professional practices face ever-mounting compliance costs. Joining two together means you can share these costs. It's a good reason to merge.

6. **Knowledge base** – almost the opposite of compliance, but arguably more important in a fast-changing sector such as law or architecture. Sharing your knowledge with others means both less spent and more learned.

7. **Customer overlap** – you supply the same people with different things. Merging means you have lots more time to find and service additional business.

8. **Premises** – your lease is running out and the other concern has space available.

9. **Plant** – merging means you can buy one big efficient machine to do the work of two smaller inefficient ones. You both benefit from the economies of scale.

10. **You know the full story** – you need to be sure there are no skeletons in the cupboard.

When you merge your business with another, only one person will remain top dog – businesses with two bosses rarely work. It will help therefore if one of the advantages of merging is that those leading the new business have complementary skills. One firm, for example, might be led by an accomplished salesperson who can win lots of new business. The other might be more delivery-focused with the leader being an engineer or professional practitioner.

When merging two businesses you also need to check the following.

- **Employment contracts** – you will need to produce one that suits both teams.
- **Pay levels** – often these are different and they need to have parity.
- **Culture** – take the best of both businesses when creating the new one.
- **Your bank** – consult them before doing the deal and make sure they are supportive.
- **Customers** – make sure that key customers are happy with what's planned.
- **Suppliers** – rationalise your list to retain the most supportive.
- **Employment law** – if there are to be casualties they should be dealt with fairly and in line with current best practice.
- **Guarantees** – make sure that you are sharing financial commitments fairly.
- **Perks** – if the other owner has a Porsche 'on the firm' and your car is more modest then you need to eliminate the danger of future disagreements.
- **Advisers** – if you have different advisers, collectively choose the one to stick with after the merger.

10 things you'll do differently the second time around

When you've sold your business, the first thing you'll want is a long holiday. Then you might decide to put into practice all you've learned and do it all again, either in the same business sector or a completely fresh one. There are ten ways in which your second business will probably be different from the first.

1. **More objective** – you'll be less idealistic and more focused on the business itself. Serial entrepreneurs are usually more stimulated by the performance of their enterprises than by what they actually make or do.

2. **People-focused** – the best businesses are those with the best people. Motivating others to deliver your vision is always easier the second time. You know how to recruit better.

3. **Tougher** – we learn from our mistakes. You're tougher and can weather the storms.

4. **Compassionate** – being aware of where others are trying to go makes you more tolerant and more willing to compromise a little. You are also older and wiser.

5. **Better funded** – you can afford to invest more the second time. That helps all round.

6. **Better networked** – you know people and people know you. It's easier when you have an established network. Your reputation will help you succeed sooner.

7. **Buy better** – you know how to buy and what to look for. You won't get ripped off.

8. **Sell more** – already successful, you have the confidence and skill to sell more successfully than you did when you first started out.

9. **Play harder** – you've perhaps enjoyed a sabbatical and appreciate the value of quality time. Life is more balanced this time round.

10. **Quit quicker** – you'll build value faster and make your exit sooner.

Most businesses in the UK are small with annual sales of less than £150,000. Only a few experience the runaway success that can deliver vast riches. Running a small business is as much a career as a quest for wealth. As with a career, you will go further faster if you:

- **move often** – selling, learning and starting again is the fastest way to grow;

- **delegate** – focus more on strategy and less on operational issues;

- **stay clean** – do not tarnish your reputation;

- **help others** – it's odd, but the more you help others the better you do yourself;

- **enjoy it** – making work fun also makes it easier – this goes for your team too!

Really successful people often build a portfolio of businesses. These will include companies that they:

- **invest in** – and support the executive team to achieve the vision;

- **own** – but which are entirely managed by trusted employees;

- **advise** – where they give their expertise freely and learn too;

- **admire** – in which they have a small role but derive much pleasure;

- **respect** – and want to help to succeed.

To keep developing your skills as an entrepreneur you should now:

- scan business books and journals and read what's best for you;

- help others, for they in return will want to help you;

- listen to reputable business speakers and ask them probing questions;

- keep a diary so that you can look back and learn from what you did;

- create a training plan for yourself and be prepared to invest in good courses.

20 Useful document templates

shortcuts for you to copy, adapt and use

Sales letters

You use sales letters to make an approach to people you think might be interested in the products or services you offer. It is more direct than advertising and can give you a better response. Here are ten important things to consider when writing sales letters.

1. **Targeting** – sales letters are not direct mail. It's better to send a few well-aimed letters than distribute thousands of poorly targeted, impersonal ones.

2. **Research** – the more you can find out about the person you are writing to then the more likely it is that they will read your letter. Use the internet to research your prospects.

3. **Personal** – people get lots of junk mail. Your letter has to be quickly seen as 'something else'. Make the letter obviously personal to the recipient.

4. **Familiarity** – older people prefer to be addressed as Mr or Mrs. Younger people are happy to be addressed as 'dear first-name'. Don't be overly familiar or too formal.

5. **Short** – the best sales letters are short and to the point. Keep to one page.

6. **Specific** – make it very clear what you are offering and why you think it's appropriate to your target. Tell them in clear terms why you have written to them. Do not use the tactic employed by large mailing houses who use phrases like 'you have been selected for'.

7. **Say what you want** – there has to be a simple call to action. Don't use euphemisms – say it like it is.

8. **Don't ask too much** – your sales letter is written to open dialogue with your prospect. People don't buy from sales letters – they simply respond to an invitation to know more.

9. **Sign it yourself** – always sign your sales letters personally and don't use black ink. If you do, people will assume it's been printed rather than handwritten.

10. **Offer choices** – let people choose how to respond. Enclose a reply envelope and provide a phone number. Offering choice increases the response rate.

Sample sales letter

Dear Mr Smith

I was browsing classic car websites the other day and noticed that you are secretary of the Anytown Triumph Herald Club. Classic cars are an interest of mine, although I have yet to buy one of my own.

My company provides embroidered shirts, baseball caps and other promotional merchandise to sports and social clubs of all kinds. I wondered if your club members would like the opportunity to wear clothing that carries your club name and logo?

Some of the clubs we serve sell our products to raise funds for the club. Others choose to sell them to members at cost because they like members to 'fly the flag' at meetings and events.

We would be delighted to work with you to design and provide garments and merchandise that your members will value and enjoy. If you could fill in and return the short questionnaire I have enclosed, I will willingly produce you a sample T-shirt without obligation. Alternatively, give me a ring if you have any specific needs or ideas you would like to discuss.

I look forward to hearing from you.

Yours sincerely

Steven Stitch

Sales letter structure

1. Name your prospect to make the letter personal.

2. Explain how you got their name and why you're writing.

3. Say what you do and why it's relevant.

4. Ask the recipient to do something and offer alternatives.

5. Sign it with your first name and family name.

6. If you promise an enclosure, don't forget to put it in!

Follow-up letters

Once you've established two-way communication with your prospect or customer, you need to keep in touch. Don't pester them but write whenever there's a specific opportunity you think would appeal to them. Here are ten examples.

1. **It's been a while** – you've written about some offer but there's been no response. It's been proven that sending up to two follow-up letters can prompt purchase. People often simply put your letter to one side or forget. No reply doesn't always mean no interest.

2. **Your next service is due** – if you maintain equipment for your customer, take the initiative and write to tell them when the next service is due.

3. **Good news** – you've just won a business award. Write and tell your customers and include a 'celebratory' offer. Equally, write it so that they win an award too!

4. **Deadlines** – we all live with them. Write to your customers when you know a significant deadline is looming. This also applies to seasonal businesses.

5. **Referral letter** – a new customer has suggested some people you might contact. Break the ice with a letter of introduction that names the person who referred them.

6. **They said no last time** – if you lose an order, wait a while and then write to ask how they're getting on with the new supplier. Things might not be working out. You need to know.

7. **You saw them in the paper** – everyone loves being pictured in the newspaper. Write to congratulate them and then introduce your offer. Few others will do this.

8. **You've a new product** – give existing customers the chance to preview new products. It makes them feel that they are important to you.

9. **You want to delegate** – as your business grows, you will want to pass some customers on to your team. Do this by letter of introduction – it avoids them feeling dumped.

10. **You're fund-raising** – it may be your job to raise money. Equally, you might simply be looking for sponsors for your first marathon. Write to your supporters and they may support you more.

Sample follow-up letter

Dear Mr Smith

It's been three months since your last purchase of our multivitamin tablets for your dog. I hope that your pet is well and that you have seen an improvement in health, vitality and condition as a result of adding our products to your animal's feed.

By our calculations you must be ready for another consignment soon. Would you like me to post some to you? The price remains the same as before, £25.00 for a box of 500 tablets. Postage and packing is free. I enclose a ready completed order form and reply paid envelope for your convenience. Alternatively you can phone or reorder via our website.

I also enclose information about our new lines of pet care products. Many customers have been asking us to widen our range and we have been happy to oblige. You can add any of these to your next order and we will cover the cost of postage.

I look forward to hearing from you.

Yours sincerely

Steven Stitch

Follow-up letter structure

1. Name your customer to make the letter personal.

2. Explain why you're writing – make it specific.

3. Spell out what it's going to cost and don't miss a new sales opportunity.

4. Make it easy to respond.

5. Sign it with your first name and family name.

6. If you promise an enclosure, don't forget to put it in!

Getting-paid letters

You've done the deal and sent the invoice. Now you need to make sure you get paid. Here are ten steps to getting your money, however reluctant the customer is to pay!

1. **Make sure your invoice is correct** – incorrect invoices can get stuck in the customers' accounts department. Make sure it's accurate and quotes their order number.

2. **Send a statement** – some people pay only on receipt of a statement. Send one at the end of each month to summarise recent transactions.

3. **Pick up the phone** – if the money's overdue, ring and ask for it. Find out what the problem is. If there is no problem you need to move on to step 4.

4. **Write a letter** – be firm and polite and make it clear when you expect to be paid.

5. **Second letter** – express disappointment that you've not seen payment and say that you will take legal action if the money is not with you by a certain date.

6. **Post a copy of your completed Small Claim's Court form** – this shows that you are serious (small claims are those less than £5,000). Write to give one more week to pay.

7. **Start court proceedings** – the court then writes to your debtor and many pay at this point. They also have to pay your court fee.

8. **Attend the hearing** – small claims are heard by a judge in his office. It is relatively informal and the judge will be friendly and fair. You are face to face with your debtor.

9. **If you win the hearing** – your debtor will be required to pay you, perhaps by instalments.

10. **If you lose the hearing** – reflect on why this happened. Was there any fault on your side? Did you fail to prepare your argument for the judge? Be honest with yourself.

Sample getting-paid letter

Dear Mr Smith

Despite sending you a statement and phoning your office to speak to you, it appears you have still not settled my invoice number 1234 (a copy of which I enclose). You have not given me any reason why you have chosen not to pay for the bricks we delivered to your site on 18th March and I must insist that you send me a cheque by return.

We accept credit cards, so if it would be more convenient to spread your payments using your credit card to settle our invoice we would allow that. You do, however, need to call in to our depot to do this.

I am very sorry that you have not managed to find time to either pay this invoice or to speak with me when I phoned. I feel we have no alternative but to start a Small Claims Court action against you should your money not be in our bank by the end of the month.

I look forward to hearing from you.

Yours sincerely

Brian Brickmaker

Getting-paid letter structure

1. Name your debtor and be polite – avoid sarcasm.

2. Outline the steps that you've already taken and enclose a copy invoice.

3. Explain what you will do if the money is not forthcoming. Offer a choice if you can.

4. End by expressing your sorrow at the situation.

5. If you promise an enclosure, don't forget to put it in!

The business plan

There is a checklist to help you prepare your business plan on page 32. Here though is an example of how the information can be presented on one page.

My one-page business plan – The Red Bus

My objectives	My goals	To make this happen I need to	And I'll do these first
What we do:	Income/profit Sales this year: £50,000 Sales next year: £150,000 Sales in 3 years' time: £400,000	• Carry more passengers • Make more money from each one • Encourage more people to travel by bus	• Change my timetable • Add some new routes • Join an environmental party
Who we do it for:	Customers No. Spend p.a. This year: 1,000 £50 Next year: 2,000 £75 In 3 years' time: 3,000 £133	• Sell newspapers • Start to do excursions • Do weekend breaks	• Open a wholesale newspaper account • Build a list of clubs and societies • Explore hotels that will give me a deal
What makes us money:	Products/services This year: One bus Next year: One bigger bus In 3 years' time: One bus plus one coach	• Trade in my bus for a bigger one • Start looking for a coach • Buy a coach in two years' time	• Start reading *Bus Weekly* • Visit a coach exhibition • Find out about finance
Where it's leading:	Investment This year I need £5,000 Next year I need £20,000 In 3 years' time I'll need £80,000	• Find more working capital • Find a leasing company to fund the bus/coach • Plan an advertising budget	• Talk to my bank and others • Join a business network • Talk to marketing firms
What's in it for me:	People This year I employ: Next year I need: In 3 years' time I'll have:	• Employ part-time drivers • Employ four part-time drivers • Employ one full-time and five part-time drivers	• Find out what other firms pay • Build a list of good drivers • Ask my two drivers who they know

Confidentiality and intellectual property

You are right to be concerned about protecting what is yours from those who might copy it. If the stakes are high, you should never cut corners but hire the best professionals you can afford. For those seeking a quick fix, here's a checklist and a draft disclosure agreement.

1. **Be pragmatic** – you can take this stuff too seriously. Remember that the cost of litigation is so high that having agreements, trade marks and patents is only half the story. Defending your rights against a large, well-resourced opponent can be prohibitive.

2. **Mind who you show** – if you've developed something new then talk to a patent agent before you show it to anyone else. Once you've shown others, it can prove impossible to patent.

3. **©** – add this symbol to everything you publish. It simply asserts that you are claiming it as copyright.

4. **TM** – this abbreviation for 'trade mark' can be added to any logo or symbol you consider your own. You don't need to register it to do this, just add a superscript ^{TM} to any print.

5. **®** – this symbol means you have a registered trade mark. You need to consult a trade mark lawyer (or be very clever) to get trade marks registered.

6. **Non-disclosure agreements** – these are most usually used when you are showing a potential associate or supplier the details of something you plan to protect by patent. Remember that you cannot patent what you have publicly disclosed.

7. **Patents** – are listed on national patent registers. You need a patent agent to help you to file a patent as the process is lengthy and complex. You can search the UK register of patents by following the link to 'find patents' here: *http://www.ipo.gov.uk/patent.htm*.

8. **Domain names** – always remember that search engines look for website content – the name of your domain is not as important as you might think. That said, it does make sense to have a domain name that links to your business or product name. Search to see what is available here: *http://www.whois.org/*.

9. **Business name** – if you're going to be a sole trader, you can pretty much choose whatever name you wish. Legally you will be 'John Smith trading as Acme Carpets' or similar. However, to avoid confusion make sure you

research carefully and do not choose a name that may get you confused with someone else. You can register almost any trading name as a 'trade mark', providing that someone else hasn't registered it already!

10. **Perspective** – your approach to trade marks, patents and the like will largely be dictated by your ambition. If you are setting out to beat the world, you need to invest in the best possible advice because much of the value of your business may rest in its intellectual property. If, on the other hand, you simply want to enjoy life and be comfortable this might not be quite so vital to your continued success. Be realistic and keep things in perspective.

Sample non-disclosure letter

CONFIDENTIAL DISCLOSURE AGREEMENT
Between: [company name and address]
and: [your name and address]

1. On the understanding that both parties are interested in meeting to consider possible collaboration in developments arising from [your name]'s intellectual property, it is agreed that all information, oral, written or otherwise, that is supplied in the course or as a result of such meeting shall be treated as confidential by the receiving party.
2. The receiving party undertakes not to use the information for any purpose, other than for the purpose of considering the said collaboration, without obtaining the written agreement of the disclosing party.
3. This Agreement applies to both technical and commercial information communicated by either party.
4. This Agreement does not apply to any information in the public domain or which the receiving party can show was either already lawfully in their possession prior to its disclosure by the other party or acquired without the involvement, either directly or indirectly, of the disclosing party.
5. Either party to this Agreement shall on request from the other return any documents or items connected with the disclosure and shall not retain any unauthorised copies or likenesses.
6. This Agreement, or the supply of information referred to in paragraph 1, does not create any licence, title or interest in respect of any intellectual property rights of the disclosing party.
7. After [numerals] years from the date hereof each party shall be relieved of all obligations under this Agreement.

Signed: [your signature]
For: [your business/trading name if relevant]
Date:

NOTE: This sample document is just that, a sample. It was reproduced by permission from *www.abettermousetrap.co.uk* where further information can also be found.

Robert Ashton

I hope you have found this book useful. The format, with practical checklists and case studies, makes it very easy to read. I've even had e-mails from dyslexic entrepreneurs telling me how the first edition was the first business book they had been able to finish!

It doesn't matter what kind of entrepreneur you are, the challenges are largely the same. You may be growing your own enterprise, or simply seeking to be more entrepreneurial in a large organisation. Many readers will be starting social enterprises too – it's a fast-growing sector.

Whatever your enterprise and whatever your motivation for reading this book, I'd like to hear from you. It is only by listening to you, by hearing how this book has helped you succeed, that I learn how I can develop my skill as a writer. I look forward to hearing from you.

Robert Ashton
robert@robertashton.co.uk
www.robertashton.co.uk

READ ON ...

Get your business off to the best possible start with Steve Parks' bestselling books for business owners and entrepreneurs.

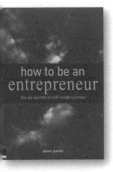

HOW TO BE AN ENTREPRENEUR

▶ 9780273708292 ▶ £12.99

This is the ultimate guide to becoming a brilliant entrepreneur. It's packed with ideas, inspiration and practical advice to help you develop the attitudes and focuses of top entrepreneurs, and make your business a success.

START YOUR BUSINESS WEEK BY WEEK

▶ 9780273694472 ▶ £14.99

Want to start your own business but don't know where to begin? Then overcome the challenges and turn your ideas into reality in just six months with this definitive week by week start up guide.

HOW TO FUND YOUR BUSINESS

▶ 9780273706243 ▶ £14.99

This is THE book to take the pain out of financing your start up! It provides the facts, figures and reassurances you need to choose the right source of funding for you and your business.

THE SMALL BUSINESS HANDBOOK

▶ 9780273695318 ▶ £18.99

This practical reference book is the perfect guide to running and growing your business. Filled with advice and guidance on all the day-to-day aspects of running your enterprise, it ensures you are well equipped to tackle every new situation that arises.

READ ON ...

Essential advice, inspiration, tips and techniques for every stage i starting up and running your own business.

FROM ACORNS

▶ 9780273712527 ▶ Caspian Woods ▶ £9.99

Packed with practical wisdom and tips from countless entrepreneurs who have been there and done it, *From Acorns* is the no nonsense guide to starting a business that every entrepreneur should have. Whether your plans are modest or on a grand scale, this book helps you get i right first time around.

THE START UP SURVIVAL GUIDE

▶ 9780273708322 ▶ Chris Lilly ▶ £12.99

This book is your small business survival guide. It sets out all the common mistakes, errors and pitfalls entrepreneurs make in every area of business, and show: you solutions for the tricky issues that you might face.

THE BEERMAT ENTREPRENEUR

▶ 9780273704546 ▶ Mike Southon ▶ £12.99

You've got a bright idea that you think just maybe, could become a brilliant business. *The Beermat Entrepreneur* takes you through all the crucial stages of starting a business that is sound, lasting and profitable. It tells you what the other books don't – the lessons that most people have to learn by bitter experience and the tricks that all entrepreneurs wish they had known when they started out.

You can buy these books in all good bookshops, or online at **www.pearson-books.com**

PEARSON
Prentice
Hall